A New Approach to Christmas Greetings

'To this gentle night, of stars and snow,
    The gilded tree and of candles glow,
Come distant voices, sounds so dear,
    To be bound in a wreath of Christmas cheer.'

Toni Schultheis

A New Approach to

Christmas Greetings

By ViAnn Oden

Anvipa Press
Goleta

Publisher's Cataloging in Publication Data

Oden, ViAnn

  A New Approach to Christmas Greetings.

  (Anvipa Christmas Ease Series)

  1. Christmas Greetings 2. Christmas Cards 3. Christmas
I. Title. II. Series.
Library of Congress Catalog Card Number: 88-70777
Printed in the United States of America

Additional Copies can be purchased from:

       Anvipa Press
       160-D N. Fairview Ave. Suite 226
       Goleta, CA 93117

or by using the Order Blanks in the back of this book.

To Lori Ellen

Daughter, Friend, Encourager

Disclaimer

A New Approach to Christmas Greetings is a guide to Christmas greetings and does not claim to be the ultimate source of such information. This book is sold with the understanding that Anvipa Press and author ViAnn Oden shall not be held liable nor responsible to any person or entity with respect to any loss or damage caused or alleged to be caused directly or indirectly by the information in this book. Although the publisher and author have made every effort to make this guide as comprehensive and accurate as possible, there may be errors both typographical and in content.

Acknowledgements

It has been my good fortune to find many helpers who contributed to this work.

I would like to express special thanks to Paul Hartloff, my editor, for making my wish come true. I owe much to my parents, Mr. and Mrs. Robert Bristol, who provided encouragement and a writer's retreat. My family, Bob, Lori, Michael, John and Matt were incredibly patient—more than once.

I also gratefully acknowledge contributions from Susan Miller, Mr. and Mrs. Michael Harrington, Mr. and Mrs. Robert Locke, Margo Chase, Mary Alice Schlueter, Toni Schultheis, Margaret Page and Cathy Carlson.

Table of Contents

Section Four:

Preface

Have you become a slave to the Christmas card habit?

Has this annual tradition lost its luster?

Do you find yourself making snap decisions just to get the job done? Are you sometimes unhappy with your final card selection, stressed over a rapidly enclosed note and frustrated over the lack of originality? Do the words "one more responsibility" echo in your ears?

Sit up straight, breathe deeply and commit yourself to a NEW AP-PROACH this year. Planning is essential when tackling most holiday tasks. Shopping for gifts without a list or cooking a turkey without seasoning would never occur to us. Yet, year after year, the tradition of sending Christmas cards and letters continues without adequate planning or new information. Take a fresh look at this holiday tradition and learn how to plan creatively and efficiently. Make sending cards delightful, not dismal— use the information in this book.

Revitalize the tradition. Customize your strategy. Save time and energy— be in control. You deserve a NEW APPROACH To CHRISTMAS GREETINGS!

 The generally accepted first Christmas card was designed in England by John Calcott Horsley in 1843.

How to Use This Book:

A New Approach to Christmas Greetings provides you with information in four subject areas. Read the following information for a description of separate sections. Then read the introductory material to each section for a more detailed description.

SECTION ONE will help you design a personal approach to Christmas cards. You will become aware of past frustrations and impulse buying while receiving information on a new approach. You will no longer feel trapped in a tradition which controls you. Choices, purchasing habits, notes and verses, signatures and addresses will help you say "Merry Christmas" with a plan. Generally accepted correspondence etiquettes, postal regulations, holiday stamps and original worksheet information are also included. This section will help you be creatively organized.

SECTION TWO opens the door to more seasonal greeting options. You are encouraged to look beyond Christmas cards and challenged to communicate through an alternative method. Guidelines and graphic art aids are included for Christmas letters, postcards and party invitations. Information on photo greetings include snapshot guidelines, commercially available borders, and suggestions for mounting your own photograph. Suggestions regarding holiday use of telephones, cassettes and videos may stimulate you to embark on totally new traditions!

SECTION THREE will encourage you to feel instantly artistic. Read this section carefully. It could be the springboard to an exciting annual hobby. By learning to use simple graphic arts tools, you can enhance or replace commercial holiday greetings with minimal effort. Interesting techniques and tools are discussed. Samples featuring creative use of picture and letter stencils, vinyl letters, transfer type, typewriters and computers. Heavy emphasis is placed on the creative use of clip art and rubber stamps. This section is required reading for the unique holiday correspondent!

SECTION FOUR is a collection of charts, lists and record-keeping forms. These worksheets have been discussed in previous sections. This is a section for personal use. Make notations in pencil and learn about your preferences in design, color and organization. Keep a complete record of holiday correspondence by using the various charts.

Section One

Christmas Cards

TAKE a moment and think:

What is your approach to Christmas cards?
Do you make impulse decisions when choosing a card?
Do you confine yourself to traditional colors and forget that
   each card has a theme?
Are you frustrated over how many to send?
Do you spend more money than you had planned?
Are you unhappy about the hours spent signing, addressing
   and mailing?
Are you trapped in a tradition?

Start now—be *in charge* of this activity!

Use the following sections. Understand the steps involved when sending Christmas greetings. Don't let the process control you. Be knowledgeable and creative and know how to:

*	Choose a card	Pick a theme that says "you". Select a color that says "new".
*	Purchase a card	Learn about new places to buy cards. Save time and money. Know where and when to shop.

*	Add verses to cards	Be creative and customize your greetings.
*	Sign and address a card	Know acceptable guidelines. Learn about exceptions.
*	Mail a card	Find out about postal regulations, colored envelopes and Christmas stamps.
*	Record your card	Discover patterns and plan greetings ahead. Use a worksheet.
*	Display your cards	Design a new approach.
*	Plan your card	Learn about the *Holiday Time Card*, designed for card senders.
*	Send fewer greetings	Terminate a habit. Enhance a tradition. Discover new options.

How to Choose Christmas Cards

"CHOICE" is a key word for today's American shopper. Individuals want to express themselves through their purchases. Christmas cards are no exception.

 The first American Christmas card was produced in the early 1850's and depicted Santa Claus and individuals pleased with receiving presents.

While traditional and religious themes continue to be available, new holiday trends are firmly outlined on the horizon. Greeting card firms, such as American Greetings, are prepared to offer new ideas using tradition as a springboard. They currently design cards with holograms, music and blinking lights. Other changes include traditional messages paired with innovative art style, cute characters, contemporary lettering or an updated color look. Whatever the style, theme or color the feelings shared continue to be warm and focused toward the recipient. The sender has a choice in expressing herself.

Hallmark Cards and Ambassador, leaders in the social expression industry, publish more than eleven million greeting cards each working day. They share the world's largest creative staff—nearly 700 artists, designers, stylists, editors and photographers create designs for greeting cards and related products.

Choosing and purchasing a Christmas card can be a delightful part of the holiday season. A small amount of forethought can eliminate frustration and enliven the tradition with new enthusiasm and satisfaction. Set aside time to plan this activity.

Annually, many people rush to their local retailer to quickly grab Christmas cards. This fast-paced ritual has reduced our appreciation for the custom. Written and illustrated communication to friends, relatives and business associates has become a holiday routine. Unfortunately, routine often promotes unimaginative traditions.

Before rushing to your local card retailer consider your personal preference. Eliminate impulse buying. Plan according to your tastes.

If you have a stack of old cards spend a few moments reviewing. Do certain cards hold your attention? Why do you like these cards? Perhaps you enjoy certain themes or colors. Do you find a particular verse especially meaningful? Hopefully, you will gain some quick insights.

At this point you have established personal guidelines for future purchases. Suppose you find yourself attracted to cards depicting winter snow scenes. Seven cards in your collection depict this theme; two of these cards seem especially appealing. You notice both are enhanced with pastel colors as opposed to traditional reds and greens. Now, you review the original stack of cards and again notice, without exception, your preference for pastels.

 Louis Prang, a German emigrant, began printing cards in Massachusetts in 1874, using a lithographic process which employed as many as twenty colors. Subjects included the Nativity, Santa Claus, children, pretty girls, birds and butterflies.

The task of choosing this year's greeting card now becomes simple. You will not be forced into impulse choices which will lead to possible frustration and disappointment. You are focused and in control of what has previously been an annual dilemma.

As you approach card retailers you can eliminate overwhelming choices. You love snow scenes and you prefer snow scenes enhanced with pastels. You can quickly scan card displays and find designs which meet your preferences. You are no longer easily distracted and find yourself confidently focused. Your final choice excites you. You are enthusiastic about sending this particular greeting to your relatives and friends. A part of you will be shared.

Don't be afraid to be unique. Shop for a way to individually express yourself. Imagine that you simply don't like any of the cards in your personal selection. You have worn the carpet thin in the Christmas card section of your local store. You have flipped through dozens of cumbersome oversized Christmas card catalogs in an attempt to find the perfect card. What happens now?

Think about yourself. What are the symbols that project you? What are your hobbies or interests? What do you do for recreation? Are you dedicated to a particular occupation?

Suppose you love North American Indian artifacts and have collected books, made jewelry or traveled extensively to Indian reservations. People know these experiences to be a part of you. Research the places that support your interest in Indian culture.

You might enjoy the Christmas greeting cards designed by Rebecca Brockway. Paper Sharks produces a line of her watercolor and oil pastels in vivid contemporary colors. These cards include hand-lettered original verse which add to the overall batik feel. Information regarding card design and Indian culture are included on the card back.

These special cards can be purchased by writing to:

    Paper Sharks
    3463 State Street
    Santa Barbara, CA 93105
    Attn: Terry Churchill

In order to eliminate annual decisions regarding themes and colors, your personal formula for selection can be used for several years. Perhaps you initially select a design depicting a lion and a lamb lying side-by-side. You may wish to send a different card each year depicting this theme. Not only do recipients begin to notice and look forward to this year's design, but you may collect an interesting display of cards which could be framed for a Christmas decoration. A lady, living off the coast of Southern California on Catalina Island, has sent cards depicting cats in neutral colors for the past twenty years. Friends and relatives look forward to her annual card reflecting on her love of the feline.

 Jonathan King, a Victorian citizen of Islington and a great collector of Christmas cards, is known to have shown a contemporary:
ten volumes of robin Christmas cards
one volume of snowmen
one volume of insects
one volume of donkeys
one volume of velvet birds
one volume of birds made of real feathers
one volume of political cards, etc.

Consider using the worksheets in Section Four when making decisions about themes and colors. These worksheets contain common themes and design ideas for Christmas cards. A list of colors is also available as an aid for those who wish to avoid the traditional red and green associated with the season.

Below is a sample section from the *Christmas Card Choosing Guide* worksheet:

Decide on the major topics that most appeal to you and place marks in the appropriate boxes. Here the Religious and Miscellaneous sections are given as examples. Then look at the more specific topics and mark those that you like. Spaces have been left in each category so that you may include other themes.

   ❏ RELIGIOUS   ❏ MISCELLANEOUS

○ Angels   ○ Bells
○ Bible/Scripture   ○ Candles
○ Church Scenes   ○ Houses
○ Lion & Lamb   ○ Fireplaces
○ Nativity   ○ Instruments
○   ○
○   ○

Have this worksheet handy when you look at and purchase your Christmas cards so that the choice will be easier.

Christmas can be celebrated using colors other than red and green. Advanced technology replaced black and white television with "full color"—perhaps the addition of new colors could enliven this season. Consider new colors when selecting cards.

Primary Red is wonderful, but so is—

Cranberry,
Fuchsia,
Mauve,
Hot Pink
and Dusty Rose.

Primary Green is wonderful, but so is—

Peacock,
Forest,
Jade,
Kelly
and Teal.

See *Christmas Color List* in Section Four.

How to Purchase Christmas Cards

PLAN the amount of money you wish to spend on greeting cards. If you are addicted to expensive quality cards know exactly how many you are willing to purchase. Mailing fewer cards may enable you to send your favorite selection. If you mail an extensive amount of cards you may wish to limit the price per card or box. In either case plan before you go shopping.

Purchasing individual cards is costly. However, if you send a limited amount of greetings, individual choices may better suit your tastes.

When sending larger amounts of cards, determine how many cards are in a box. It will vary with the manufacturer. Plan your list to take advantage of price.

You can often send more greetings for the same price using boxed cards. Use the following chart to estimate the amount of cards needed and the total price. Remember to include mailing costs or hand deliver to reduce mailing expense.

Number of cards to send	10	20	30	40	50	60	70	80	90	100
Individual/Unboxed $1/ea.	$10	$20	$30	$40	$50	$60	$70	$80	$90	$100
Box of 20 @ $4/box	$4	$4	$8	$8	$12	$12	$16	$16	$20	$20
Box of 20 @ $5/box	$5	$5	$10	$10	$15	$15	$20	$20	$25	$25
Box of 20 @ $6/box	$6	$6	$12	$12	$18	$18	$24	$24	$30	$30
Box of 20 @ $8/box	$8	$8	$16	$16	$24	$24	$32	$32	$40	$40
Box of 20 @ $10/box	$10	$10	$20	$20	$30	$30	$40	$40	$50	$50
Box of 20 @ $12/box	$12	$12	$24	$24	$36	$36	$48	$48	$60	$60
Box of 20 @ $14/box	$14	$14	$28	$28	$42	$42	$56	$56	$70	$70
Box of 20 @ $16/box	$16	$16	$32	$32	$48	$48	$64	$64	$80	$80
Box of 20 @ $20/box	$20	$20	$40	$40	$60	$60	$80	$80	$100	$100

Boxed cards are often covered with clear plastic lids. Don't be afraid to slip off the cover and carefully examine the top card. Do you like the typeface used for the verse? If you plan to sign your cards with a felt or fountain pen is the paper surface suitable? Certain inks will smear or fade on glossy paper— think about your writing tool now!

By 1915, personal photographs on postcards began to phase out and make way for a new trend. World War I cut off access to German postcard greetings; cards in envelopes were now in style. Most of the new cards were imported from France and England and for the first time boxes of cards were available for greeters.

When to Purchase Christmas Cards

CARDS can be purchased earlier each fall from retailers and catalogs. Discounts often apply if cards are bought before a certain date. This incentive plan helps the purchaser avoid holiday rushes.

If you buy cards after Christmas for the following year, substantial discounts often apply. It is common to see one-half price sales on Christmas cards December 26th. Those quality cards you had hoped to purchase before Christmas may now be yours at a reasonable price.

Some card retailers are following a new sale trend. Cards are marked down a few days before Christmas in hopes of reducing inventory which must be stored until the following season. If you are prepared to leave time for this activity so near the holiday, the choices may be limited, but so is the price.

Where to Purchase Christmas Cards

CHRISTMAS cards can be purchased in department stores, drug stores, variety stores, stationery stores, printing shops, card shops, museums and by catalog.

Department stores, stationery stores and printers usually have large sample books from different companies. You may order cards in different price ranges and in different amounts. For an additional charge your card can be imprinted with your name. This approach can save time while adding a more formal feeling to the greeting. Remember that discounts often apply if cards are purchased before a certain date in the fall of each year.

While many people would never forsake the annual tradition of exchanging Christmas cards, more than a few contemplate trimming their lists or donating the usual amount spent for cards to a charity.

The National Charities Information Bureau can help a donor make a better gift-giving decision. They currently publish a bi-monthly newsletter entitled *Wise Giving Guide* which rates not-for-profit organizations based on eight standards of philanthropy. A copy of this newsletter may be obtained by request at the following address for $1.00 a single copy:

> National Charities Information Bureau
> 19 Union Square West
> New York, NY 10003

Another meaningful approach might include a change in your shopping patterns. Rather than replace the tradition consider purchasing cards from non-profit organizations such as the following:

★ United Nations
   International Children's
   Emergency Fund (UNICEF)

   Cards and gifts may be obtained by
   writing for a catalog entitled:

   The Winter Collection
   U.S. Committee for UNICEF
   331 East 38th Street
   New York, NY 10016
   Tel: 1-800-228-1666 or 1-800-642-8787 (Nebraska)

★ The National Wildlife Federation

Write them at:

The National Wildlife Federation
8925 Leesburg Pike
Vienna, VA 22180

On a local level consider purchasing cards at various types of:

- museums
- botanical gardens
- non-profit hospital gift shops
- other favorite non-profit organizations

The Christmas season tugs at our memories and pulls us back to childhood scenes. We are frequently reminded of needy children whose holidays may be dismal. Consider sponsoring a child through a non-profit organization. Write for information or call:

Christian Children's Fund
P.O. Box 26511
Richmond, VA 23261
Tel: 1-800-241-8444

Foster Parents Plan
157 Plan Way
Warwick, RI 02886
Tel: 1-800-556-7918

Mission International
2000 E. Red Bridge Road
Box 419055
Kansas City, MO 64141
Tel: 1-800-821-3089

Save the Children
50 Wilton Road
Westport, CT 06880
Tel: 1-800-243-5075

World Vision
P.O. Box O
Pasadena, CA 91109
Tel: 1-800-445-9887

 "Poor children" were frequently the subject of Christmas cards during the second half of the Victorian Era. Artists hoped to evoke sympathy for hard-working, ragged children. By 1926, an American card expert noted that current cards do not "even intimate the idea that unhappiness exists.... They would fall quickly by the wayside, for everyone is intent on scattering sunshine and joy."

How to Use Words with Christmas Cards

Just sending a greeting card with your signature below the printed text is not a proper form of communication. Greeting cards are fine in themselves, but they are not complete. They must be personalized. They must include a written message, however small.

The Amy Vanderbilt Complete Book of Etiquette
Revised and Expanded by Letitia Baldrige

Add a brief message to the card. Perhaps it will only be a question, quotation or comment, but do include a handwritten note such as:

> Dear ViAnn:
> We are doing fine. I am teaching 3rd grade at a school in Arcadia— a class of 16! It's great! Dave is driving his "new" '76 Ford pickup truck. Allison is driving us crazy! Aren't teenagers fun? Hope all of you are well and happy.
>
> Love,
> Dennis & Margaret
> Dave and Allison

Or, if you will see your friends later during the holiday season:

> "We miss you and look forward to an enjoyable New Years Eve together."

The sentiments or verses inside a card range from traditional greetings like "Joy" to lengthy quotes. It may affect your choice depending on who will receive the card. A box of cards appropriate for business associates may lack the necessary warmth for relatives. Only you can make the decision. Consider purchasing a different box of cards for each audience or buy individual cards for selected individuals.

 The earliest known American Christmas greeting was sent by businessman Richard H. Pease to his customers about 1851. This card depicted a family celebrating Christmas with punch and plum pudding and included the merchant's store name in prominent display-lettering advertising "Pease's Great Variety Store in the Temple of Fancy".

A recent trend toward no verse or blank cards has allowed senders to personalize greetings. Your own original enclosure verses can be inserted. Use a book of quotations as inspiration. Consult any of the following texts readily available at your local library.

Bartlett's Familiar Quotations
John Bartlett

Dictionary of Quotations
Bergen Evans

The Home Book of Quotations (Classical and Modern)
Burton Stevenson

The International Thesaurus of Quotations
Rhoda Thomas Tripp

When using any of the above reference books remember to look under subject headings besides "Christmas" in the book index. For example, try some of these— holiday, holly, mistletoe, Santa and snow. *The Home Book of Quotations* lists thirty-two references to the word "snow" alone— then it continues with *snow-broth, snow-hid, snow-wreath, snowballs, snowdrift, snowdrop* and *snowflake*. Cross referencing is sure to provide you with that needed quotation.

One of the most popular early American cards contained this sentiment message framed in holly:

I am thinking of you today because it is Christmas
  and I wish you Happiness
And tomorrow, because it will be the day after Christmas,
  I shall still wish you Happiness...
And so on through the year.

Christmas cards which you've received in previous years are another good source of quotation ideas. Greeting card companies receive thousands of verse submissions annually. If you need an idea for an original verse consider the choices of these companies as a starting point.

And if nostalgia is your hallmark you might enjoy using early Christmas sentiments on blank cards or Christmas letters. On the following pages are samples of verses which appeared on cards as early as 1876.

"Remember, remember!
Thus carols December,
And do not forget Christmas
    Greetings to send."
        (Anonymous, 1876.)

"A Happy Christmas!
To thee my wishes wing their eager flight,
Swift as my messenger, and not less bright."
        (U.S.A., 1877.)

"Christmas comes! While you are sleeping,
In the holy Angel's keeping,
He around your bed is creeping,
And within the curtains peeping,
Leaving for all good girls and boys
Such merry games, and pretty toys."
        (Prang, 1878.)

"Hark the word
    By Christmas spoken—
Let the sword
    Of war be broken."

"Let the wrath
    Of battle cease—
Christmas hath
    No word but—Peace."
        (Sentiment by Eden Hooper
        on an Eyre and Spottiswoode
        card of the 1870's.)

"Peace and love and joy abide
In your home this Christmas tide."
(1880's.)

"A happy Christmas to my Friend,
And countless Blessings, without end."
(1878.)

"I send the sweetest maid
With letter unto thee,
Of Christmas greeting on the seal,
'Remember me.'"
"So sweet is she, my friend,
I'm more than half afraid
That you'll forget me and will think
But of the maid!"
(Kate Greenaway.)

"We seem too busy every day
To say the things we want to say;
Out deepest thoughts we seem to hide
Until we reach the Christmas-tide.
'Tis then we send to friends again
In happy words the Old Refrain—
'A Very Merry Christmas'."
(U.S.A. sentiment, 1920's.)

"Never a Christmas morning,
Never the Old Year ends,
But somebody thinks of somebody,
Old days, old times, old friends!"
(U.S.A., 1920's.)

"Only a simple greeting,
But it brings a wish sincere
For the happiest kind of a Christmas
And the finest sort of a year."
(1920's.)

The Dear Old Tree
BY LUELLA WILSON SMITH

There's a dear old tree, an evergreen tree,
And it blossoms once a year.
'Tis loaded with fruit from top to root,
And it brings to all good cheer.

For it's blossoms bright are small candles white
And it's fruit is dolls and toys.
And they all are free for both you and me
If we're good little girls & boys.

Keep the following points in mind when writing an original verse on a card or letter:

- ❧ Rhyme is nice. *Keep verse short and avoid overworked rhyming words.*
- ❧ Rhyme is not a necessity. *Unrhymed verse and everyday language are often preferable.*
- ❧ Read your verse aloud. *Listen for rhythm.*
- ❧ Customize your greeting. *Use familiar names.*

 During the First World War, Americans added a kiss to their Christmas greetings. Cards decorated with stars and stripes had a special gum-coated space where lips could be impressed on the surface. The printed verse read:

> For Uncle Sam you're fighting
> And it makes me love you so
> That I send a kiss in the space above
> To take wherever you go!

How to Sign Christmas Cards

IN AN ISSUE of *Spectator,* December 31, 1948, Harold Nicolson describes a unique way to add a signature to a Christmas card.

"This delightful method," he relates was devised by a "versatile and inventive friend... The moment he receives a Christmas card he puts it in an envelope and posts it to someone else. If the card has been inscribed by some affectionate hand, like 'Love from Pamela' or 'With the compliments of Messrs. Rickshawe, Court Hairdressers,' he does not trouble to erase these inscriptions. He merely adds the words 'and Richard.' He contends that this method...gives added pleasure to his friends. Not only do they get their cards, but they are left wondering who Pamela may be."

Guidelines for signing greeting cards are listed below:

From A Married couple:

>Dave and Cyndee Ellis
>>or
>Cyndee and Dave Ellis

A Family:

>The Ian Millers

With one child:

>Ian and Susan Miller and Sean

With children:

>The Ian Millers - All Five
>>or
>The Millers - Ian, Susan, Sean, Eric and Kevin

A Second Family (with children from a previous marriage):

>Greg and Joanie Littler
>and all the family
>>or
>Greg and Joanie Littler
>and children

The Amy Vanderbilt Complete Book of Etiquette
Revised and Expanded by Letitia Baldrige

If your first name is somewhat common avoid undesirable "guessing games" for your card recipient. Almost everyone has received a card reading "love, Jim" or "love, Susan" — only to wonder for the remainder of the holiday season who Jim and Susan might be.

On a more humorous note, a Cherry Valley, California homemaker used her Christmas card signature to solicit a quick and friendly phone call from distanced friends. She signed her family Christmas cards in the following manner:

The Ogden Family
Robert, Ann, Lori, Michael, John, Matthew and Twins

Because Mrs. Ogden had delivered Matthew the previous spring everyone called to find out about the twins—who of course did not exist.

How to Address Christmas Cards

FOLLOW accepted guidelines for addressing Christmas mail:

Addressee	Form
Married Couple	Mr. and Mrs. John Roberts Street address and possible apt. no. City, state, and zip code
Married Couple (when wife has retained maiden name)	Mr. John Roberts and Ms. Loren Smith Street address and possible apt. no. City, state, and zip code
Married Couple (sharing each other's last names)	Mr. and Mrs. John Smith-Roberts Street address and possible apt. no. City, state, and zip code

Family

Mr. and Mrs. Robert Locke and Family
Street address and possible apt. no.
City, state, and zip code
or
Mr. and Mrs. Robert Locke
Street address and possible apt. no.
City, state, and zip code

add to the inside of the card:

Love to the children
(Michael and Allison), too.

How to address cards to children: Miss to Ms. & Master to Mr.

A girl from infancy	Miss Lori Allen
A girl after entering high school	Ms. Lori Allen
A boy until approximately eight years old	Master Michael Owen
A boy between eight years and entering high school	Michael Owen
A boy after entering high school	Mr. Michael Owen

Although the previous suggestions cover most situations, trick questions are inevitable. For instance, how do you address mail to a divorced woman? Unless you know what she prefers, "Miss", "Mrs.", or "Ms.", make a reasonable guess or try checking with someone who knows her well.

Another common question regarding the proper use of "Senior", "Junior" and "III" is answered in the following quote from *Miss Manners* by Judith Martin:

> ...the answer is that the eldest living holder of a family name does not use a suffix (a widow may use 'Senior' to distinguish herself from her daughter-in-law) and that 'Junior' and 'III' move up when 'Senior' dies.

How to Record Christmas Cards

KEEP a record of the Christmas cards you send each year. This will help you purchase the correct amount of cards next season. Keep a record of cards you receive. This will help you streamline your list if you plan on sending fewer greetings next year.

Use the *Christmas Card Record*, found in Section Four, in the following way:

1. Print names and addresses— avoid unnecessary mailing errors.
2. Record your card as sent— circle appropriate year.
3. Record cards received from same address— circle appropriate year.

When using the chart the first time, arrange cards to be sent alphabetically by last name and record the addresses and the year sent on chart.

| Name: |
| Street: |
| City: _____ State: _____ |
| Country: _____ Zip: _____ |
| Sent: 19__   19__   19__   19__   19__ |
| Received: 19__   19__   19__   19__   19__ |

How to Mail Christmas Cards

THE U.S. POSTAL SERVICE encourages individuals to mail domestic Christmas correspondence between Thanksgiving and December 15th. Overseas mail should be sent in November. Only metered mail needs to be bundled in packets of five or more pieces. Due to new optical scanning systems the post office would prefer:

- Light colored envelopes— dark colored envelopes are much less desirable due to readability.
- Typed address (center front)— however, block printing and legible handwriting are definitely acceptable.
- Return address (front upper left corner)— not on back flap.
- Sealed envelopes— use envelope adhesive, tape, sealing wax or stickers. Avoid staples.

First-class Christmas stamps are generally available by late October. You may choose from two designs, religious and contemporary, which are sold in sheets of 50 and 100 depending on stamp size. The Stamp Advisory Committee, made up of non-postal private citizens, reviews and selects stamp designs two to three years prior to issue.

In 1938, Postmaster Earl S. Johnson designed a rubber stamp Christmas tree with the inscription MERRY CHRISTMAS FROM THE LITTLE TOWN OF BETHLEHEM. The stamp, called a cachet, became a tradition for Bethlehem, Connecticut. The post office has continued to offer this service with a new stamp each year.

These special Christmas Stamps cannot be purchased, but the newest impression is available each December. If you want the cachet to appear on your Christmas cards follow these steps:

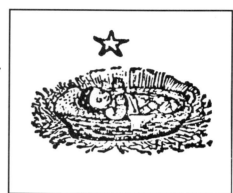

1. Address, seal and affix postage to each of your Christmas cards.
2. Put cards in box and wrap securely.
3. Write a letter to Bethlehem, Postmaster requesting:
   a. that Christmas cachet be stamped on enclosed cards.
   b. that Christmas cards be mailed in Bethlehem.

   NOTE: Add a "written hug"— this service is a step beyond the call of duty. "Thank-you" and "please" should be included without compromise.

4. Address letter to: Postmaster, Bethlehem, CT 06751 Remember to stamp letter and place on outside of box.
5. Place correct amount of postage on box and mail.

Included here are samples of cachets from past years. It may be worth your time to follow the steps above. Not everyone gets a Christmas card from *Bethlehem!*

If you wish to mail your Christmas letters or cards with a North Pole postmark, send then to:

> Santa's Workshop
> North Pole, CO 80809
> Tel: 1-303-684-9432

This post office even sends directions for Christmas mailing on cute holiday letterhead. A reprint of this information follows:

If you wish to mail your Christmas letters/cards with a North Pole postmark:

✳   The envelopes should not be red, as our meter ink is
    red and we cannot use red on red;

You may stamp the letters yourself or...

✳   You may enclose your check (payable to Santa's
    Workshop for the correct amount of postage;

✳   Please package your letters/cards in a box and send
    them to us by U.P.S. or U.S. Mail;

✳   We must receive them by December 1, in order for
    them to be postmarked by December 10 (in time for
    pre-Christmas delivery);

✳   They will be postmarked by December 10, unless you
    specify another time for them to be mailed;

✳   All foreign mail should be postmarked by November
    29.

   North Pole Post Office receives thousands of letters to be mailed
each season...we ask that you allow time for your packaged letters
to get to us prior to December 1.

A pictorial cancel from Santa Claus, IN (zipcode: 47579-9998) may
be obtained in a similar fashion. Be sure and request the special
Christmas cancel as it is hand-stamped. This post office mails within a
day or two of receipt.

How to Display Christmas Cards

CHRISTMAS greetings can be used as more than messages. They make wonderful holiday decorations. Share the joy of seasonal correspondence with holiday visitors.

- Arrange your cards on bookcase shelves, the mantel or arch them over a window. Use your imagination. Add greens in the background to enhance their color and design.
- Tape the cards to ribbon and use two or more of these card lines on a door or wall to form a design, like a star or Christmas tree. You can fill in the center of the design as more Christmas mail arrives.
- Make a permanent card tree using heavy wire or wooden dowels. Cover the branches with florist tape. Tape, pin or hang your cards from a tree.

In addition to the above suggestions, write to Taylor Gifts for information regarding their greeting card wreath. This company retails a giant (43.5" H x 36" W) corrugated cardboard wreath which has slots for fifty cards and a red bow at the bottom. It's a clever way to decorate the wall and display cards at the same time.

> Taylor Gifts
> 355 East Conestoga Road
> P. O. Box 206
> Wayne, PA   19087-0206
> Tel: 1-215-293-3688

Current, Inc., a mail order company specializing in cards, package wraps, ribbon and assorted gift items, retails a card garland to display holiday greetings. You simply insert your cards in posterboard hangers, lace them together with green yarn and hang on wall, staircase railing or mantel. The set includes forty-eight hangers and eighteen feet of yarn, comes with instructions and is reasonably priced.

Current also sells a *Santa's Sleigh Christmas Card Garland*, a giant wall decoration that displays thirty-six cards on the reins of Santa's sleigh. It includes a designed posterboard sleigh (14.5" H x 11.25" W) and reindeer (each about 10.5" H x 7" W) with fifteen feet of red yarn for the reins. For more information on the above items or a complete catalog, write or call toll free:

Current, Inc.
The Current Building
Colorado Springs, CO   80941-0001
Tel: 1-800-525-7170

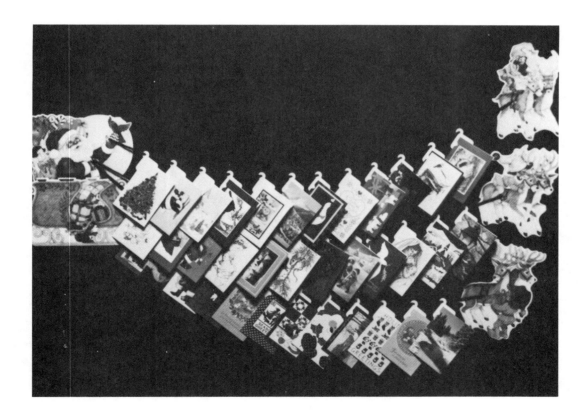

Christmas Cards and Time

CHOOSING, purchasing and mailing Christmas cards takes time. As with any task, determine how much time you can reasonably delegate to holiday greetings.

Different lifestyles often dictate the amount of time spent on any project. Avoid unnecessary feelings of guilt if you decide to limit the number of cards you send; experience satisfaction with limited mailing.

Christmas cards are usually mailed in December before Christmas Day. Examine your holiday schedule and determine the need for a possible change.

If you have too many activities during the month of December:

★ Consider mailing your cards after Christmas. *A warm greeting has no deadline.*

★ Consider sending cards every other year. *Annual Christmas card mailing is a tradition—not a law.*

★ Consider sending some cards on another holiday. *Mailboxes are available throughout the year.*

If you delegate time to sending cards, carefully estimate your available hours. This project can easily grow from a delightful expectation to a dreary burden. The *Holiday Time Card* for Christmas greetings in Section Four will help you estimate the time you spend choosing, purchasing, signing, addressing, stamping, sealing and mailing Christmas cards. Use the *Time Card* as illustrated below:

	Browse through old cards	Determine number to send	Select and purchase	Sign and address	Seal and stamp	Record cards	Mail	Total Time
Budgeted								
Actual								

Share card responsiblities. You may wish to choose and purchase your own card, but family members or friends can help with signing, addressing, stamping, sealing and mailing. Share the joy! Use the chart in Section Four to delegate activities.

An article in Home Chat in 1895 described Queen Victoria's use of Christmas cards— "Not only does she procure at great expense cards for all her royal relatives— and we know how numerous they are, but she buys not less than thousands to send to her neighbours at Windsor and Osborne". The writer continued by describing a nativity design, ten inches wide and eight inches deep, which the Queen had ordered for her relatives in Europe - "The whole is got up in a most lavish manner and leaves the beholder in wonder as to how the Christmas card of the present day can be improved upon." This same article describes the cards sent by the wife of U.S. President Cleveland as "peculiarly interesting, in as much as they are all of more or less Puritan nature or time, and are unequalled for chaste simplicity and good taste."

How to Send Fewer Christmas Cards

TAKE a serious look at the names on your Christmas card list. Does the list seem unnecessarily long? Does the length of the list make this holiday task a burden? Consider eliminating some of the names on your list by reviewing your card-sending habits.

★ You may want to eliminate sending cards to people who have not sent you a card for the past two years. *They no longer feel the obligation.*

★ Remove names of people living in your town. *These cards may be habits, not greetings.*

★ Reduce your list by omitting the names of those people who will receive gifts from you. *One act of thoughtfulness may be enough.*

★ Consider deleting the names of people you see everyday. *Wish them a Merry Christmas in person!*

Who's left? People who live a distance from you and truly look forward to your greeting.

Suggestion: If you reduce your card list significantly and wish to inform close friends and associates, notice might be issued through a final card. Insert a small notice in the card which might read:

In lieu of sending Christmas cards to our many beloved friends we will donate the usual amount spent to our church. We continue to wish you many merry times during future Christmas Seasons.

or

We plan to send fewer Christmas greetings in the years ahead. Please know that we continue to think of you during this season.

 Even early Victorians found it difficult to write the necessary volume of Christmas letter to friends and relatives in other towns and villages. Writing paper decorated with Christmas themes was available for the holdays, but all required a personal handwritten message. The newly efficient postal systems had created a new dilemma for individuals; more greetings could now be sent.

Section Two

Creative Alternatives to Christmas Cards

CHRISTMAS CARDS are an excellent way to say "Merry Christmas", but greetings need not be confined to cards. Letters, postcards and invitations can serve equally well as seasonal greeting vehicles.

Don't underestimate your control. Communicate yourself through the method you like best. Say "Merry Christmas" with:

*	Christmas Letters	Be aware of guidelines. Learn where to purchase special borders, decorative corners, holiday letterheads, and graphic tape.
*	Postcards	Be brief, warm and economical. Make your own.
*	Photo greetings	Make a lasting impression with a simple picture. Know the guidelines.

*	Party invitations	Use special party stamps. Look for unusual forms. Be creative.
*	Modern Forms	Use a telegram, mailgram or computer greeting. Think about telephones, cassettes and videos.
*	Cards as Gifts	Easy to mail enclosures make the difference.

Christmas Letters

CHRISTMAS letters and notes are frequently the only annual written communication between distanced friends and relatives. Receiving a personal letter is an enjoyable experience.

> There is nothing within the range of human emotions that cannot be expressed by the reflective written word. It is sad that the world of instant communications has made us so lazy that we are losing the ability to communicate our real selves to each other on paper.
>
> *The Amy Vanderbilt Complete Book of Etiquette*
> Revised and Expanded by Letitia Baldrige

Too many Christmas letters contain lengthy descriptions of the years past events emphasizing tight schedules. Receiving a letter which reads like a corporate calendar is neither welcome nor entertaining.

 Sir Henry Cole, an organized and busy man, who wanted to save time on his 1843 Christmas letters, requested that John Calcott Holsley design a printed card.

If your Christmas letter resembles this actual correspondence received by a West Coast resident, rewrite now. Very few people would appreciate receiving such a greeting. However, it adds unintentional humor when comparing samples of Christmas letters.

Dear Friends, It seems like it is that time of year again. Time to stay in touch with all of our friends and to wish everyone a Merry Christmas. We hope all of you are having a nice winter.

S— is having an incredible year as a seventh grader. One of his drawings of a bird has been on display at the junior high for the past seven weeks. There are only four chosen from any one school (all area junior and senior highs are represented) so now we know how talented he really is. He has also spent many hours practicing his trumpet and is doing very well. The band director even called one night to emphasize how well he is doing and how much he has improved. This marvelous boy also topped off his quarter by bringing home a report card with straight A's and perfect grades in citizenship.

E— has also been very active this winter. He has been a member of the church junior choir (he has such a beautiful voice) and the church junior bell choir. He is so musical. He and S— have also spent many hours learning about lambs for their 4H Project. He participated in his school's jog-a-thon and raised almost $70. This enabled him to win a new basketball. He's a super salesman, just like his daddy. He also went to the Little League try-outs. He did just super. He caught all the balls thrown to him, hit the ball far, and was one of the few boys his age who could pitch strikes. We know he is going to be a star on his team. He also was in the Cub Scout BMX bike day. There were boys from 2nd, 3rd, 4th and 5th grades. He had the highest score of anyone. Isn't that great talent and great ability.

K— is getting to be such a big boy. He lost his first baby tooth and that was an exciting day for the whole family. ... His coach frequently commented about how fast he runs. We're sure he is going to be a terrific ballplayer also. To top off all these marvelous activities, all three boys recently went to the dentist and none had a cavity. We must be doing something right. Imagine that!

...My activities include cooking, cleaning, washing, chauffeuring, delivering books to shut-ins, working on a Youth Advisory Board, playing piano for the junior choir, substituting in kindergarten, being a den mother, baseball fan and interior decorator. I don't know how I do it all. I even spent a day in the hospital with a kidney stone, but bounced right back to entertain my sister-in-law and a friend the next day.

The end of last November saw us heading off to Oak Glen...

The last four paragraphs of the letter have been deleted in sympathy of the reader.

Jeff Kunerth from the Knight-Ridder News Service recently said: "Verbosity roams the landscape of language unbridled...."

When composing a Christmas Letter, omit needless words. Scan your sentences and paragraphs on a rough draft and rewrite if necessary.

Avoid the elaborate, the pretentious, the coy, and the cute. Do not be tempted by a twenty-dollar word when there is a ten-center handy, ready and able.

(The Elements of Style; William Strunk Jr. and E.B. White)

The following letter was sent by a newlywed couple in 1986. The letter, designed on a computer is friendly and informative but appropriately concise.

GREETINGS!!

The latest breaking news since Kerry and Michael became a unit.

For those of you who haven't heard from us since the big event, (that would be the wedding) this is a little of what we have been up to....

The honeymoon was the perfect way to unwind after all the hoopla and planning of the wedding. We visited the wine country in Napa, drove across Utah to visit friends (where, by the way, Michael got to use his hang glider for a few good flights) then through Wyoming to Colorado to visit my folks.

I rented out my house and we made the move to Santa Cruz in mid-August. We spent some time fixing up the new house and working in the yard before Michael started school and I went to work.

This year Michael is majoring in Economics to finish his degree in Environmental Studies ... interesting and challenging!

I am working for a computer software company called Quantumwave as assistant to the Marketing Manager. It is a good way for me to use my marketing skills while at the same time increasing my knowledge of computers...the way of the future.

We will be feathering a new nest as of January 1, 4558 Harrington Dr., Santa Cruz, CA 54908. We hope to stay there longer as the feathering process takes a good deal of energy. We find married life to be agreeable and enjoy our time together. We wish you a wonderful holiday season and a full and happy new year.

MERRY CHRISTMAS!!!

Consider sending a Christmas letter using the following guidelines.

Use good quality paper, available in a variety of colors

Things to do today:

Call Stationery store!

1. Center letter.
2. Leave good margins on both sides (1" to 1.5").
3. Skip a line between paragraphs.

Handwrite, unless you judge your handwriting illegible. Then type WITHOUT regret.

Write out full date.

December 15, 1988

Suggestions:

★ Select highlights or incidents which hallmarked your year. Describe their importance.

★ Avoid paragraphs of inflated family cameos. Be reasonable when sharing the accomplishments of your spouse or offspring.

★ Humor has its place. Share a laughable incident or tasteful joke.

★ Emotions are okay. Many feelings can be shared through the written word that are difficult to express face to face.

If you decide to share the same information with several people, consider photocopying your letter. Use a good quality machine. Remember machines will allow you to copy your letter on colored paper.

An attractive letter can be designed by using Border Boards manufactured by the Graphic Products Corporation. Below are samples of the designs currently available. Because the border is printed on blue graph paper, you may write on the lines and maintain exact margins.

The blue lines will not reproduce on a copy machine. Your finished letter will be attractive and readable.

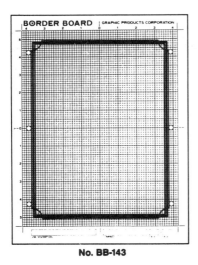

No. BB-143

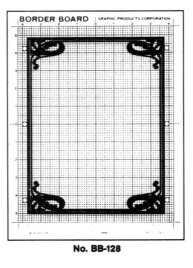

No. BB-128

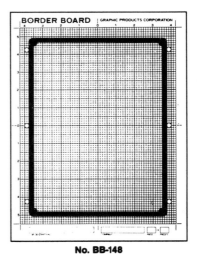

No. BB-148

Graphic Products Corporation
3601 Edison Place
Rolling Meadows, IL 60008-1062

Letraset USA will provide you with another graphic shortcut—decorative corners. Instant Lettering corners can be transferred to your Christmas letter with a burnisher. Using this method, characters can be added to your correspondence for minimal cost. You may place an order through art, drafting and engineering stores across the country. For the name of the Letraset dealer in your area please contact:

Letraset
40 Eisenhower Drive
Paramus, NJ 07653
Tel: 1-800-526-9073

More ideas include:

★ Attractive copyright free art can be added to enhance your Christmas letter. See Section Three for examples and addresses on where to obtain clip art and how to use it.

★ Add the artwork of a child to your Christmas letter and experience the joy of *an original*. Below is a cover sheet to a Christmas letter. It was drawn in felt pen by a five year-old and reproduced on a copy machine.

★ Photo-Fantasies Unlimited will personalize stationery products for you. Send them your favorite photo and any phrase you wish including name and address. They will print your photo in black ink on your choice of paper color. To obtain a catalog, write:

Photo-Fantasies Unlimited
7939 Limerick Avenue
Canoga Park, CA 91306.

★ Add charting and graphic art tape to your Christmas letter. Decorative lines can be formed with this tape to make borders or divide sections. Use blue-lined graph paper for your letter. The lines will provide guides for placing the tape but will not reproduce on a copy machine. Use a fine cutting knife such as an X-acto to cut tape at the end of desired lines. Check your local art, drafting, or engineering section at local stores. Formaline makes tape in a holly design which is 1/4 inch wide (#7331K).

★ Add a holiday sticker. Card and specialty shops retail a vast assortment of colorful stickers. You are limited only by your imagination.

★ Rubber Stamp your letter. See Section Three for suggestions on how to rubber stamp holiday greetings.

★ Liven up your Christmas letters with colorful pre-printed holiday stationery. They're compatible with most copiers and printing processes if you wish duplicates.

★ Carlson Craft also produces a computer Christmas letterhead including matching envelopes. Designs include colorful ribbons and holly, religious borders and snow scenes. If you have a computer, this company may end your Christmas letter hassles forever. Continuous Christmas letterhead (9.5" W x 11" H) is available to fit computer printers and word processing equipment. The perforated margins provide clean, smooth edges making it difficult to tell that letters are generated by computer or word processor. Write to:

Carlson Craft
P.O. Box 8700
North Mankato, MN   56002-8700

Postcards

A FRIENDLY Christmas greeting can be sent economically on a postcard. Museums and card shops often display boxes of Christmas postcards in assorted designs. A brief, warm message can be added and mailing charges are less than sending cards enclosed in envelopes.

Consider making your own postcards on medium to heavyweight paper or buy blank postcards from your local post office. Write message and verse with bright colored pens. Enhance with rubber stamp images, transfer type, transfer art, stencils or vinyl letters. For a more detailed description of these personal touches, see Section Three.

If you make your own postcard, remember U.S. Postal requirements regarding size:

MINIMUM SIZE: 3 1/2" X 5"
If your card is smaller, it won't be sent.

MAXIMUM SIZE: 4 1/4" X 6"
If your card is larger, first class postage will be required.

There is no such thing as correct size when referring to Christmas cards. George Buday reports in *The History of the Christmas Card* that the smallest card known to him was a grain of rice. It was given to H.R.H. the Duke of Windsor in 1929. Buday describes the card as "stuck on a paste board of 3 1/4 by 2 inches and the text on the actual grain of rice, inscribed in Indian ink, reading:

'To His Royal Highness
The Prince of Wales
Sincere Christmas Greetings
From The
Joseph G. Gillott Pen Co.,
London, England
Season 1929.'"

If you love Santa Claus postcards, don't miss the reproduction of Beverly Port's *Antique Santa Post Cards* published by Hobby House Press, Inc. Fifty-four cards, originally published in the early 1900's, are included in Volumes I and II. All postcards can be removed from the book by folding along perforations.

Because the more unusual Santa Claus postcards are fast disappearing into advanced collections, this may be the only way to see and enjoy the variety of treatments artists have given to the popular fellow. Each card's origin is described on the message side of the postcard.

Thin or rotund, happy or stern and Oh' the fabulous colors!
No, Santa was not always dressed in red with white fur trim.

Antique Santa Post Cards
Beverly Port

The inside cover of *Antique Santa Post Cards* suggests ten clever uses for these postcards. Volume I and volume II are available by writing to:

Hobby House Press, Inc.
900 Frederick Street
Cumberland, MD 21502

If children are on your holiday mailing list, consider sending a very special holiday message on a Postal Puzzle. Choose from a dozen colorful designs. Postal Puzzles have fifteen pieces and are individually shrink-wrapped. Add a first class stamp and it is ready to mail! For ordering information write to:

Seakrafter
404A Bayview St.
Yarmouth, ME 04096

Photo Greetings

LASTING impressions can be communicated by a good photo greeting. As your life changes yearly, a simple photograph may tell more than a lengthy Christmas letter.

Photo greetings are generally available at film processors by mid-November. Take your photo negative to an outlet and choose a special holiday border and greeting for your print. If desired your name can usually be imprinted on the card.

If you prefer to make the photo greeting yourself, mount your favorite picture on medium to heavyweight paper. Add your Christmas message on the border or reverse side. Have fun enhancing the card with lettering, using the numerous methods mentioned in this book.

If you wish to send a commercially printed card, simply enclose a photo or mount it on the left-hand interior opposite the verse.

Take time to plan your greeting. Every picture is not suitable for framing and the same rule applies to photo greetings. Be selective and follow a few simple guidelines:

☛ Natural light is wonderful. Plan a photo session outdoors and hope for an overcast day. Late morning and afternoon light is preferable; avoid high noon.

☛ Indoor pictures taken with a camera with built-in flash produce "red-eye". If you are determined to photograph indoors, use a blue photo bulb and a clip-on shade. Reflect the light off a white wall, sheet or board. Experiment with heights and angles.

☛ Simple backgrounds do not distract from the subject. Make use of plain fences, full bushes and walls without decoration.

☛ Your subject should feel casual. Consider less formal clothing— smiles may come easier.

☛ Fill the frame by moving close to your subject. The background should only provide a border.

☛ Keep camera steady. A tripod or shutter release cable may be helpful.

☛ Take many pictures. Don't be afraid to shoot a whole roll or more. That's how professionals get the perfect shot.

 In 1902, George Eastman's Kodak Company offered post-card-stock photographic paper to amateur photographers. Now picture-snappers could print their own negatives to produce Christmas postcards. The demand for this type of greeting increased and by 1906, Kodak advertised its own service of printing postcards from customer's negatives.

If you like to shop by mail, order a catalog from Exposures. This company carries photo Christmas cards in both horizontal and vertical designs. Border trims include diamond, reindeer, pear tree, snowflake and ribbon motifs. All you do is insert your favorite photo. They even retail a photo gluestick which is dripless and water soluble.

Note for Christmas card collectors: Exposures also retails a beautiful hunter-green, bonded leather scrapbook with "Christmas Collection" stamped in gold on the cover. This album comes with twenty-four archival pages to organize Christmas photo greetings. It is bound screw-and-post style, for easy expansion. A matching caddy is also available to keep cards from getting lost before you have a chance to mount them. Write to:

Exposures
475 Oberlin Avenue South
Lakewood, NJ 08701
Tel: 1-800-222-4947 or 1-201-370-8110 (New Jersey)

 According to the Photo Marketing Association International, Americans take approximately twelve billion pictures annually. If you spread them out, the entire land area of the United States would be covered 134 times. If you stacked them end-to-end, your "photo pile" would reach to the moon and back three and a half times!

Party Invitations

TO AVOID double mailings during the busy holiday season, include party invitations with your Christmas card. You may write the necessary information on the inside cover opposite the verse or enclose a separate written invitation.

A lawyer and his wife in Santa Barbara, California, make clever use of a standard law form as a party invitation enclosure.

Attornerys for <u>Amicus Curiae</u>

SUPERIOR PARTY OF THE STATE OF CALIFORNIA FOR THE COUNTY OF SANTA CLAUSE

JON B. AND SALLY M. KANE)
)
Hostors,)
)
invite) No. 10th ANNUAL
) NOTICE OF PARTY
DOES I - ??, to be named within,)
)
Hostees.)

TO ADDRESSEE HEREIN AND TO THEIR SPOUSE OR COMPANION OF RECORD:

PLEASE TAKE NOTICE that on December 13, 19--, beginning at 8:00 p.m. and continuing thereafter from hour to hour until completed, Hostors JON AND SALLY KANE, will give their Tenth (10th) annual Christmas party at their home located at 777 Holiday Hill, San Nicolas, California.
Hosts respectfully request your appearance at said place at the time and date set forth above.

DATED: December 1, 19--

This idea of using professional forms need not be limited to lawyers. Whatever your profession might be—doctor, engineer, musician, artist or laborer—there may be some sort of form which could be adapted for use as a party invitation.

If you wish to avoid more writing and would like to include your party information on the inside of the card, Stampa Barbara makes a large rubber stamp titled "Let's Celebrate". You simply rubber stamp your invitation in any ink color and fill in the specific details by hand.

Stampa Barbara
Studio 20 * El Paseo
Santa Barbara, CA 93101
Tel: 1-805-962-4077

Modern Forms of Christmas Greetings

CONSIDER sending a unique Christmas greeting using a telegram, or or mailgram. For approximately $13.00, a message can be delivered by Western Union. Call their toll-free number for additional information (1-800-988-7426) or look up in your local telephone directory.

1. Call for rates
2. Carefully write out your message
3. Count words in your message
4. Determine cost (delete unnecessary words)
5. Obtain recipient's address
6. Call Western Union 1-800-988-7426
7. Charge to your phone number or credit card

WESTERN UNION RATE CHART

MESSAGE TYPE	DELIVERY			RATES
	WHERE	WHEN	BY WHOM	
Telegram	50 States Guam US Virgin Islands	Same Day	Messenger or phone (followed by written message)	$12.95 for 1-10 words 55¢/ each additional word; $10.95 for physical delivery
Overnight Telegram	50 States Guam US Virgin Islands	Next Day	Messenger or phone (followed by written message)	$11.95 for 1-10 words 40¢/ each additional word
Mailgram	50 States, Canada Puerto Rico US Virgin Islands	Next Day	Mail	$12.95 for first 1-50 words; $3.95 for each additional 1-50 words

Keepsake telegrams with Christmas designs can be ordered for an additional $5.00.

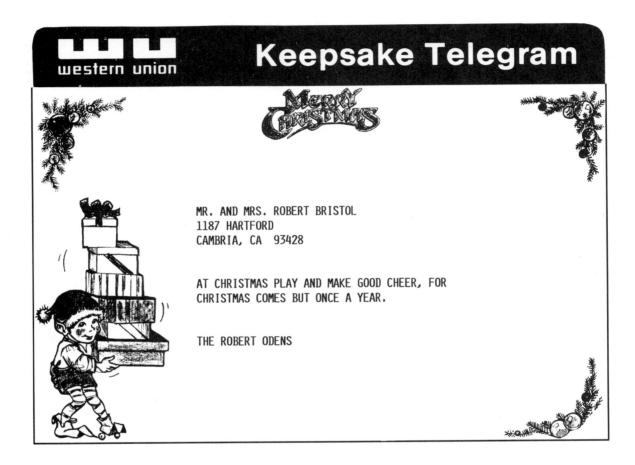

Singing telegrams can be delivered anywhere in the United States on the same day requested. The operator sings the message and a written copy is then mailed. The cost is approximately $20.00. Unfortunately, these singing messages are no longer hand-delivered.

 Prior to the First World War, six inch "talking-machine records" were sent in decorated boxes to greet the recipient in baritone. War dictated an abrupt halt to this new tradition, but Austria and Germany revived the idea with cardboard gramaphone "postcard records" reproducing the tune of "Heilige Nacht" (Silent Night).

How to send unwritten greetings:

★　Personally wish someone a "Merry Christmas"—
　　cards are not necessary for everyone you know.
★　Send a cassette—your voice may sound better than a
　　Christmas carol to friends or relatives.
★　Ship a video—remember the old saying—"a picture is
　　worth a thousand words."
★　Use your telephone—a warm, holiday chat could be a
　　relaxed experience for both parties.

Christmas Cards as Gifts

SAVE time and postage on packaging by including a gift with your
card. Think thin! Many items are too bulky for mailing in a card. Consider these suggestions and develop a list of your own. It could save
you hours of needless shopping. You can eliminate package wrapping
altogether.

Easy-to-mail enclosures:

★　Magazine subscription announcements. Check the
　　periodical list at your local library under subject
　　index.

★　Gift certificates. Department stores are great, but
　　remember restaurants, bookstores, art supply stores,
　　sporting goods shops, florists, and fitness centers.

★　Theater tickets. This can include live performances
　　or movies. Consider your recipient's tastes.

★   Stamps. Check with local stamp dealers or the post office. Designs are unlimited.

★   U.S. Savings Bonds, shares of stock or personal checks. You can't miss with these.

Ways to Personalize Christmas Greetings

MANY PEOPLE who feel they are not artistic depend on printed greetings to express their feelings. The following section suggests ways that "would be" artists can enhance or even replace commercial greetings with minimal effort.

You do not need to be an expert to add pictures or beautiful lettering to your holiday correspondence. The following sections introduce ways to address envelopes, include verses, create designs, embellish and sign cards by using readily available methods. Accelerated skills are not required. Simply follow directions carefully and make use of easy-to-obtain tools:

   *   Stencils   Letters and designs.

*	Vinyl Letters	Extremely easy, incredibly professional.
*	Transfer Type	Instant printed letters.
*	Typewriter or Computer	Unique art tools which are too often ignored.
*	Felt Markers or Fountain Pens	Experiment with calligraphy. Elegant handwriting is not a requirement.
*	Clip Art	Copyright free and available to make you an artist.
*	Rubber Stamps	Unlimited letters and designs for cards, envelopes, etc.

Stencils

STENCILS are an excellent way to print designs or letters. The un-printed portion is masked and the ink or paint fills in the available opening on the selected printing surface.

 Published Victorian Christmas cards were not immediate-ly popular. People continued to make and decorate their own greetings until the 1860's. As printing techniques and postal systems improved, commercially produced cards gained acceptance.

Letters can be stenciled by simply applying colored pens or pencils through cut-out holes. The samples below show how letters can be represented in a variety of ways:

Simple outline using stencil

Filled-in stencil outline

Filled-in background

Shadow lettering on one side

The JOY stencil design is No. 955 Berol RapiDesign 5/8" stencil. A free catalog of the complete RAPIDESIGN line of templates and lettering guides is available by writing to:

> Berol USA
> Eagle Road
> Danbury, CT 06810

Letter stencils can be purchased almost anywhere. Zippy-Sign by Zipatone are stencil lettering guides in Roman and Gothic type styles, ranging in size from 3/4" to 6".

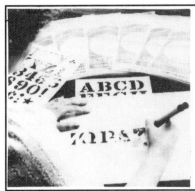

Make signs in half the time. Zipatone's Zippy-Sign Gothic Stencils are made of 10mil oil board 8" x 10" in size. The oiled board is clean and dry and keeps the markered edge sharp. This eliminates the outlining step. Just: (1) pencil a guideline; and (2) fill the letters in directly with a marker. The stencils are hole punched for easy storage in a binder.

GOTHIC STENCILS

DESCRIPTION		ORDER NUMBER	PRICE
½"	Gothic & Roman	X111050	
¾"	Gothic	X222075	
1"	Gothic	X222100	
1½"	Gothic	X222150	
2"	Gothic	X222200	
2½"	Gothic	X222250	
3"	Gothic	X222300	
4"	Gothic	X222400	
6"	Gothic	X222600	

Larger Letters or Designs:

When attempting larger letters or designs, you may also use water based paints such as poster paint. These can be applied with a stencil brush (a stiff bristled brush which holds a minimum of paint) or a toothbrush. In addition, pressurized spray paints or pressurized spray snow create interesting results.

Follow these simple steps:

1. Place card paper (medium weight) on newspaper.
2. Place stencil on card in chosen design position.
3. Pour small amount of paint onto paper plate.
   Toothbrush: Add enough water to give the paint a cream-like consistency.
4. Stencil brush: Dip into paint color. Dab brush tip on paper towel to remove excess paint. Keep brush fairly dry.
   Toothbrush: Apply paint mixture to toothbrush with watercolor brush.
5. Press stencil down firmly on paper to prevent paint from seeping under edges.

6. Stencil brush: Brush with gentle quick strokes from the outside of the cutout edge to the center of each hole. Try for a brushed look, not a solid color.
Toothbrush: Pull bristles toward you with index finger, release and let paint spatter through stencil cutout.
Spray paint or spray snow: Spray lightly.
7. Remove stencil carefully.

Stencil Art produces the two design books from which the sample holiday stencils were obtained. The Christmas Book (No. 301) and Symbols of Religion (No. 502) can be ordered by writing to:

> Stencil Art Publishing Company
> 2071 Emerson Street Unit 16
> Jacksonville, FL 32207
> Tel: 1-904-398-1420.

Custom-made templates are available for specialized or repetitive stencil needs. To obtain a price quotation from Berol, send a drawing or specification with quantity desired to:

> Berol - RapiDesign
> P.O. Box 990
> San Fernando, CA 91340

Vinyl Letters

PROFESSIONAL results can be added to your holiday correspondence with vinyl letters. These letters are extremely easy to use, simply:

1. Sketch design on scratch paper concentrating on illustration and letter placement.
2. Place light blue pencil guidelines for final letter positioning on selected paper.
3. Peel excess backing material from letter sheet.
4. Remove letters with blade of art knife.
5. Place carefully on guidelines.
6. Rub in place.
7. Carefully erase guidelines.

The following example of vinyl lettering was created with white letters (N O E L) from Chartpack. Cursive lettering was done with a Speedball artist's pen and white Pelikan drawing ink.

Chartpack makes a contemporary lettering style in seven colors. Letters range in size from 1/4" to 6". They also make symbol sheets with circles, stars, squares, triangles and checkmarks.

Consider designing Christmas letterhead for your holiday stationery, postcard headings and invitations. If you are not concerned about letter color, your original lettering can be copied on colored papers. Consider doing a reversal. Use white letters on a dark background. Your design will look professional.

 Early Victorian cards were printed on paper and sometimes enhanced with satin and fringed silk borders. Stars, fans, and other shapes were popular. Also available, were embossed, jeweled, stand-up and "squeaking cards."

Transfer Type

ANOTHER WAY to add names, headlines or greetings to correspondence is "instant lettering" or transfer type. Sheets of letters can be purchased in a wide variety of styles and sizes at art supply stores.

Sapphire

ABCDEFGHIJKLM
1234567890 &?!£$

Serifa

abcdefghijklmnopqrstuvwxyz

These letters require some patience but the results are worth the extra effort. Proceed as follows:

1. Prepare surface by lightly ruling in pencil. If your work will be photocopied, use blue pencil guide lines which do not reproduce.
2. Remove protective backing sheet and position letter on pencil line.
3. Rub each letter with pencil or burnisher. If you make a mistake, letter can be removed with masking, scotch, adhesive tapes or pencil eraser.
4. Peel transfer sheet back carefully making sure each letter is fully transferred.

These photographs, provided by Letraset, show you how to use dry transfer lettering sheets.

When doing simple lettering for Christmas correspondence, you will be amazed at how these products contribute to your creations.

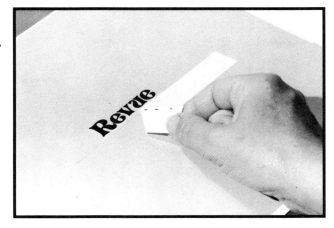

Special Note: How to Center Letters and Words

1. Trace individual letters on transfer sheet to form complete word or phrase.
2. Place the tracing on the surface of your card or letter.
3. Push a small pin through tracing paper at alignment points to form a guide for your instant letters.
4. Remove tracing paper and line up transfer letters using pin holes a guide marks.

Some dry transfer lettering sheets have a built-in spacing system. Letraset refers to theirs as an "optical spacing system". It is available on standard range lettering sheets to assist new and infrequent users.

If you plan on using one name, phrase or design repeatedly, custom made transfer sheets (measuring 10" by 13") can be ordered from Cello-Tak. Sheets are available in five colors with a 50 sheet minimum. You can design your own sheet or provide a "rough" and they will do the rest.

Letraset will also produce custom letters, symbols, and drawings on a dry transfer sheet. These special sheets are most useful when using a Christmas symbol or design repetitively or when short runs make printing impractical.

In addition to custom letters and symbols, Christmas motifs and decorations can also be transferred. Shown are samples from Letraset transfer sheets, numbers 4119, 4236 and 4110.

You might also consider using decorative initials by Letraset. The following are Letraset Decorative Initials transfer sheet numbers 4066. 4227 and 4228.

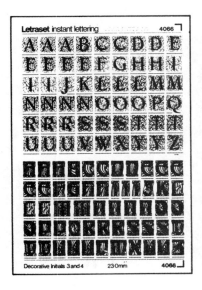 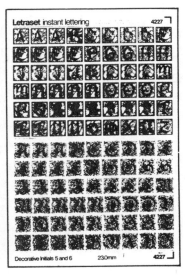 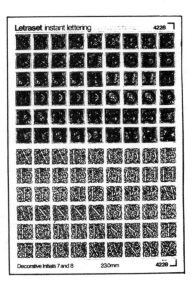

The following illustrations were taken from *The Compendium of Illustrations in the Public Domain* compiled by Harold H. Hart. The art in this book is copyright-free (see Clip Art Section). Letters were transferred using Letraset Nevison Casual.

LÖVE

is å Christmås

Bléssing

For more information on obtaining transfer type contact:

Zipatone, Inc.
150 Fencl Lane
Hillside, IL   60l62

Letraset USA
40 Eisenhower Drive
Paramus, NJ   07652

Cello-Tak
35 Alabama Avenue
Island Park, NY   11558

Typewriter or Computer Lettering

A TYPEWRITER or computer might be the art tool you've been ignoring. Unique personal designs can be created with minimal effort.

Try typing on white paper and photocopy the design on colored papers. Don't be afraid to cut and paste freely! Remember your childhood. Mount your creations on quality drawing papers, construction paper, foils or flocked papers.

Study the samples in

```
A SAVIOR UNTO YOU IS BORN THIS DAY
UNTO YOU IS BORN THIS DAY A SAVIOR
A SAVIOR UNTO YOU IS BORN THIS DAY
UNTO YOU IS BORN THIS, DAY A SAVIOR
A SAVIOR UNTO YOU IS BORN THIS DAY
UNTO YOU IS BORN THIS DAY A SAVIOR
A SAVIOR UNTO YOU IS BORN THIS DAY
UNTO YOU IS BORN THIS DAY A SAVIOR
A SAVIOR UNTO YOU IS BORN THIS DAY
UNTO YOU IS BORN THIS DAY A SAVIOR
UNTO YOU IS BORN THIS DAY A SAVIOR
A SAVIOR UNTO YOU IS BORN THIS DAY
UNTO YOU IS BORN THIS DAY A SAVIOR
```

this section before you begin to type. Notice the spacing between letters. Tightly-packed words create a more intense mood than words or letters with extra spacing. "Bold-facing" (darkening) certain words causes them to stand apart from the text and appear separate. Your computer has a special command for this purpose, but your typewriter can do the job— simply type over the copy you wish to stand out.

Use family names and unique or traditional Christmas phases. Repetition of words or phrases is the key to these designs. Consult the information on verses in Section One for more ideas. Experiment freely.

```
P e a c e P e a c e P e a c e P e a c e P e a c e
P e a c e P e a c e P e a c e P e a c e P e a c e
P e a c e P e a c e P e a c e P e a c e P e a c e
P e a c e P e a c e P e a c e P e a c e P e a c e
P e a c e P e a c e P e a c e P e a c e P e a c e
P e a c e P e a c e P e a c e P e a c e P e a c e
P e a c e P e a c e P e a c e P e a c e P e a c e
P e a c e P e a c e P e a c e P e a c e P e a c e
P e a c e P e a c e P e a c e P e a c e P e a c e
P e a c e P e a c e P e a c e P e a c e P e a c e
P e a c e P e a c e P e a c e P e a c e P e a c e
P e a c e P e a c e P e a c e P e a c e P e a c e
P e a c e P e a c e P e a c e P e a c e P e a c e
P e a c e P e a c e P e a c e P e a c e P e a c e
P e a c e P e a c e P e a c e P e a c e P e a c e
P e a c e P e a c e P e a c e P e a c e P e a c e
P e a c e P e a c e P e a c e P e a c e P e a c e
P e a c e P e a c e P e a c e P e a c e P e a c e
P e a c e P e a c e P e a c e P e a c e P e a c e
```

Prior to the first designed Christmas card, all purpose greeting cards were sometimes used to avoid lengthy handwritten messages. The sender simply inserted the word "Christmas" at the appropriate blank space.

Calligraphy

CALLIGRAPHY is usually thought of as the art of beautiful, elegant handwriting as exhibited by correct formation of letters. In China, Japan, and Korea, calligraphy is revered as highly as painting or sculpture. However, *Webster's New Collegiate Dictionary* defines calligraphy as "fair or elegant writing or penmanship".

 During the reign of Queen Anne, it was common practice for children to write Christmas pieces recognized and valued as handwriting specimens. Some sheets had engraved borders and sold in English shops until 1840.

If your handwriting is reasonably legible, consider using the following tools in lettering holiday correspondence.

- ball point pen. Remember, colors are legal.
- felt tip markers. Available in many colors and different scents.
- lettering and drawing pens. Add instant flair with colorful inks using these fountain pens with interchangeable points.

Don't be afraid to experiment. You may have more talent than you realize. Below are samples of handwriting on holiday correspondence making use of the tools mentioned.

These samples were done by Mary Alice Schlueter whose is a member of the Society for Calligraphy. Her works have been exhibited at the Faulkner Gallery in Santa Barbara, Brand Library in Glendale, Museum of North Orange County in Fullerton, Thousand Oaks Library, Golden West College in

Huntington Beach, Special Collections Department of the San Francisco Public Library and in Offenbach, West Germany. Her studio is located in the foothills of Santa Barbara.

The greeting card design below was done with a dip pen.

The following name and address was done with a felt tip pen and a fountain pen.

If you wish to pursue the art of calligraphy, specialized classes are available in most cities or consult your library for books on this art. If you simply want to have fun and leave the art to the experts, consider purchasing Binney & Smith's Crayola® Creative Lettering® kit, which "makes colorful calligraphy easy". Included in the kit are creative lettering markers, instructional booklet, parchment papers, and guide sheets. The markers come in single, double and triple chisel tips. Crayola® Creative Lettering® kit is available at many mass merchandisers, department stores and variety stores. The results are remarkable.

Letters can be dressed up quickly with dots, curves or wiggles. Experiment with simple techniques and smile at your results.

Try adding dots at the points of your letters. Slant your letters slightly in different directions. Don't be concerned if your letters are not perfectly uniform in size.

Add a small poinsettia to the letters by using a cluster of dots to portray the flower.

 The poinsettia made its first appearance on American Christmas cards early in the twentieth century—a bright rival for holly and mistletoe.

Plain dots can also be added with script.

Use a wiggle and create a letter that looks softer than snow.

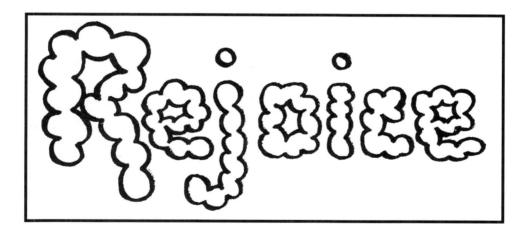

If you feel a pattern is absolutely necessary, consult *Special Effects and Topical Alphabets: 100 Complete Fonts* selected and arranged by Don X. Solo. A copy of this Dover Archives Series publication can be ordered through your local bookseller. The following samples show fonts which could be used to head Christmas letters or personalize cards. A complete alphabet for each font is printed on a full page. Make several copies of each page to insure enough copies of each letter. Now you can use a blue pencil, which will not photocopy, to create lines on your master letter or card and arrange individually cut letters to spell your greeting. Once you are happy with the layout, use rubber cement or tape to secure individual letters to master. Hide tape under cut out letters to avoid shadows when photocopying. See Clip Art section for a more detailed guide.

You might also enjoy experimenting with a flair. The samples shown are from Arthur Baker's book entitled *New Calligraphic Ornaments and Flourishes* (Dover Publications, Inc.) This clip art book contains a twenty-five page section of beautiful horizontal ornaments, arrows, and unique pointing hands. Designs among the 264 ornaments and flourishes include frames, ovals swirls, spirals, flowers and hearts. These calligraphic broad pen designs are ideal for Christmas letters and cards .

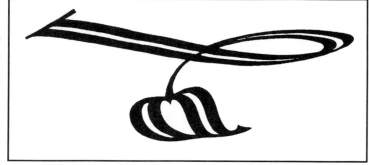

For additional resources write to:

> John Neal, Bookseller
> 1833 Spring Garden Street
> Greensboro, NC 27403

Inquire about the Letter Arts Book Club. There are no required purchases and no books will be sent unless ordered. For a small yearly membership, you will receive six mailings per year, reduced prices on many books and a calligraphic keepsake broadside!

Clip Art

PERHAPS YOU would like a sprig of holly or a rendering of Old St. Nick on the corner of your Christmas letter. Don't despair, you need not be a professional artist.

Commercial drawings are available for your use which can be reprinted without permission. Select your art from ready-to-use, copyright-free design books. Add special interest to your greeting by following these steps:

1. Begin with your own ideas. If you want to enhance a Christmas letter, write the letter first. If you are designing a Christmas card, write the greeting first. Remember, letters can be written with stencils, transfer type, calligraphy, etc.
2. Choose a piece of clip art from a commercial book.
3. Photocopy the page which includes the illustration you wish to use.
4. Cut out selection from copied sheet. Clip as near the edge of the design as possible.
5. Attach the cutout to your original page using glue, tape, rubber cement, or paste.
6. Admire your creation. You now have a master.
7. Make one test photocopy to check for quality. If the first copy you make has a shadow or lines around your illustration, use "white out" typing correction fluid to delete. Continue to use this copy as a master.
8. Now, photocopy your master, as many times as you wish. Remember, colored paper can be used in many machines. Bright greetings are a possibility using this method. Use white paper for your master copy.

Early Christmas art by Thomas Nast is available in many copyright-free clip art books.

To obtain this art, check your local art supply, school supply and book stores or write the following publishers:

Artmaster
Clip Art Catalog
500 N. Claremont Blvd.
Claremont, CA 91711

Dover Publications Inc.
Department DA
31 East 2nd Street
Mineola, NY 11501

Dynamic Graphic, Inc.
Clipper Creative Art Service
Peoria, IL 61614

Volk Clip Art
P.O. Box 72
Pleasantville, NJ 08232

Ready-to-use Christmas Borders on Layout Grids designed by Ed Sibbett Jr. is a wonderful collection of copyright-free, decorative borders featuring dozens of festive motifs for the holiday season. This book features twenty-four full-page and sixteen half-page frames printed on nonreproducible-blue background grids. You can type or write your letter with borders picturing holly, evergreen, ornaments, bells, poinsettias, etc. published by Dover Publications.

NOTE: Add felt pen coloring, glitter, or sequins to clip art. Consider cutting out your copied design and mounting on heavier colored paper.

 In 1880, Louis Prang began sponsoring open competition for Christmas card design with a first prize of $1000. Noted judges of the day included John LaFarge and Louis C. Tiffany. Cards produced by Prang are now highly prized by collectors.

Rubber Stamps

EVEN IF YOU can't draw circles, arcs, or angles, or print your name legibly, you can still be called artistic. Choose from among hundreds of Christmas designs on rubber stamps and create an unlimited variety of greetings. Rubber stamp your favorite designs on cards, envelopes, letters or invitations.

You will need:

★ Rubber stamps in Christmas designs. See list of suppliers at end of this section.
★ Inkpads in variety of colors. You can even buy rainbow ink pads with a spectrum of color.
★ Paper. Experiment! Smooth paper gives a clear impression. Glossy paper yields an excellent image, but takes longer to dry.

Following are ideas for using Christmas rubber stamps on holiday correspondence. The original stamps are made and provided by Stampa Barbara.

Stamp a greeting:

This rubber stamp of a Christmas tree without ornaments could be used to make greeting cards.

Individual ornaments have been stamped on the tree for decorations. Since inkpads can be purchased in many colors, this tree design has unlimited possibilities.

Stamp borders on Christmas letters:

When purchasing rubber stamps, choose designs which interlock.

Stamp a postcard:

This holiday house is stamped on a stock glossy postcard. Felt tip pens, glitter glue and embossing powders can be added.

Stamp a complete Nativity:

Arrange the wisemen, sheperds, angel and animals to create your own design.

 By 1884 the Florentine triptych (a three part card) featured elaborate scenes. The Holy Family was often depicted in the center, surrrounded by patriarchs, prophets, shepherds, adoring kings and singing angels.

If you decide to use rubber stamps to enhance your Christmas correspondence, consider purchasing *The Rubber Stamp Album*, by Joni K. Miller and Lowry Thompson from Workman Publishing, New York. It will tell you where to buy rubber stamps and how to use them.

Also, phone or visit:

Stampa Barbara
Studio 20 * El Paseo
Santa Barbara, CA 93101
Tel: 1-805-962-4077

This store offers more than forty thousand rubber stamps from over 120 companies. They have the finest selection available anywhere in the world. They also retail glossy blank greeting cards with envelopes, bordered blank postcards, stamping guides, glitter glue, and embossing powders which you sprinkle onto wet ink for a special engraved look.

Christmas rubber stamps can also be purchased from:

All Night Media Box
P.O. Box 2666
San Anselmo, CA 94960

Hero Arts
P.O. Box 5234
Berkeley, CA 9403

Inkadinkado
105 South St.
Boston, MA 02111

Section Four

Christmas Card
Time-Saving
Tools

USE the tools in this section to add order and fun to Christmas card selection and mailing. You may wish to add your own ideas and should feel free to add notes in the margin.

Keep this section handy as a source book each holiday season. The worksheets are guided activities which will help you explore your personal tastes and interests. Remember to take this book with you when card shopping.

Consider using a pencil for the Christmas card record. Name and address changes can be made with less hassle.

Enjoy Section Four—don't be confined by it. It is designed so that you can have fun while taking a new approach to Christmas greetings.

Christmas Card Choosing Guide

Decide on the major topics that most appeal to you and place marks in the appropriate boxes. Spaces have been left in each category so that you may include other themes.

☐ GREENERY

- ○ Garlands
- ○ Holly
- ○ Ivy
- ○ Pine Cones
- ○ Pine Trees
- ○ Poinsettias
- ○ Roses
- ○ Wreaths
- ○
- ○

☐ WILDLIFE & DOMESTIC ANIMALS

- ○ Birds
- ○
- ○
- ○

Note: Check Designs from:

National Wildlife Federation
1412 16th Street
Washington D.C.   20036-2266

☐ WINTER SCENES

- ○ Carolers
- ○ Carriage Scenes
- ○ Churches in Snow
- ○ Frozen Ponds
- ○ Ice Skating
- ○ Snow Covered Pine Trees
- ○ Sleigh Scenes
- ○ Snow-capped Mountains
- ○
- ○

☐ HUMOROUS & NOVELTY

UNLIMITED:
The majority include animals performing a wide variety of tasks; for example, polar bears making penguin trees and bears dressed as Santa Claus. Choose your favorites:

- ○
- ○
- ○

☐ SANTA CLAUS

"Santa" performing a variety of Holiday tasks. Which most appeals to you?

- ○
- ○
- ○

☐ PHOTOGRAPHIC

This includes family portraits. Be creative.

- ○ Formal Family
- ○ Recreational Family
- ○
- ○

☐ RELIGIOUS

- ○ Angels
- ○ Bible/Scripture
- ○ Church Scenes
- ○ Lion & Lamb
- ○ Nativity
- ○
- ○

☐ MISCELLANEOUS

- ○ Bells
- ○ Candles
- ○ Houses
- ○ Fireplaces
- ○ Instruments
- ○
- ○

Christmas Color List

Christmas can be more than "RED AND GREEN". Use the list below if you wish to consider other colors (or combinations of colors).

Silver	Black	Brown
Gray	Camel	Putty
Peacock	Forest	Azure
Navy	Blue	Lapis
Maize	Pink	Hot Pink
Mauve	Sable	Cranberry
Lilac	Burgundy	Rose
Raspberry	Fuchsia	Turquoise
Poppy	Yellow	Charcoal
Purple	Lavender	Aqua
Plum	Cobalt	Jade
Grape	Orange	Peach

Holiday Time Card

	Browse through old cards	Determine number to send	Select and purchase	Sign and address	Seal and stamp	Record cards	Mail	Total Time
Budgeted								
Actual								
Budgeted								
Actual								
Budgeted								
Actual								
Budgeted								
Actual								

Share the Joy

Year: _____

Choose & Purchase: _____

Sign & Add Note: _____

Address: _____

Stamp: _____

Record: _____

Seal: _____

Mail: _____

Year: _____

Choose & Purchase: _____

Sign & Add Note: _____

Address: _____

Stamp: _____

Record: _____

Seal: _____

Mail: _____

CHRISTMAS CARD RECORD

Name: _____

Street: _____

City: _____ State: _____

Country: _____ Zip: _____

Sent: 19__ 19__ 19__ 19__ 19__

Received: 19__ 19__ 19__ 19__ 19__

Name: _____

Street: _____

City: _____ State: _____

Country: _____ Zip: _____

Sent: 19__ 19__ 19__ 19__ 19__

Received: 19__ 19__ 19__ 19__ 19__

Name: _____

Street: _____

City: _____ State: _____

Country: _____ Zip: _____

Sent: 19__ 19__ 19__ 19__ 19__

Received: 19__ 19__ 19__ 19__ 19__

Name: _____

Street: _____

City: _____ State: _____

Country: _____ Zip: _____

Sent: 19__ 19__ 19__ 19__ 19__

Received: 19__ 19__ 19__ 19__ 19__

Name: _____

Street: _____

City: _____ State: _____

Country: _____ Zip: _____

Sent: 19__ 19__ 19__ 19__ 19__

Received: 19__ 19__ 19__ 19__ 19__

Name: _____

Street: _____

City: _____ State: _____

Country: _____ Zip: _____

Sent: 19__ 19__ 19__ 19__ 19__

Received: 19__ 19__ 19__ 19__ 19__

Name: _____

Street: _____

City: _____ State: _____

Country: _____ Zip: _____

Sent: 19__ 19__ 19__ 19__ 19__

Received: 19__ 19__ 19__ 19__ 19__

Name: _____

Street: _____

City: _____ State: _____

Country: _____ Zip: _____

Sent: 19__ 19__ 19__ 19__ 19__

Received: 19__ 19__ 19__ 19__ 19__

Name: _____

Street: _____

City: _____ State: _____

Country: _____ Zip: _____

Sent: 19__ 19__ 19__ 19__ 19__

Received: 19__ 19__ 19__ 19__ 19__

Name: _____

Street: _____

City: _____ State: _____

Country: _____ Zip: _____

Sent: 19__ 19__ 19__ 19__ 19__

Received: 19__ 19__ 19__ 19__ 19__

CHRISTMAS CARD RECORD

Name: _____
Street: _____
City: _____ State: _____
Country: _____ Zip: _____
Sent: 19__ 19__ 19__ 19__ 19__
Received: 19__ 19__ 19__ 19__ 19__

Name: _____
Street: _____
City: _____ State: _____
Country: _____ Zip: _____
Sent: 19__ 19__ 19__ 19__ 19__
Received: 19__ 19__ 19__ 19__ 19__

Name: _____
Street: _____
City: _____ State: _____
Country: _____ Zip: _____
Sent: 19__ 19__ 19__ 19__ 19__
Received: 19__ 19__ 19__ 19__ 19__

Name: _____
Street: _____
City: _____ State: _____
Country: _____ Zip: _____
Sent: 19__ 19__ 19__ 19__ 19__
Received: 19__ 19__ 19__ 19__ 19__

Name: _____
Street: _____
City: _____ State: _____
Country: _____ Zip: _____
Sent: 19__ 19__ 19__ 19__ 19__
Received: 19__ 19__ 19__ 19__ 19__

Name: _____
Street: _____
City: _____ State: _____
Country: _____ Zip: _____
Sent: 19__ 19__ 19__ 19__ 19__
Received: 19__ 19__ 19__ 19__ 19__

Name: _____
Street: _____
City: _____ State: _____
Country: _____ Zip: _____
Sent: 19__ 19__ 19__ 19__ 19__
Received: 19__ 19__ 19__ 19__ 19__

Name: _____
Street: _____
City: _____ State: _____
Country: _____ Zip: _____
Sent: 19__ 19__ 19__ 19__ 19__
Received: 19__ 19__ 19__ 19__ 19__

Name: _____
Street: _____
City: _____ State: _____
Country: _____ Zip: _____
Sent: 19__ 19__ 19__ 19__ 19__
Received: 19__ 19__ 19__ 19__ 19__

Name: _____
Street: _____
City: _____ State: _____
Country: _____ Zip: _____
Sent: 19__ 19__ 19__ 19__ 19__
Received: 19__ 19__ 19__ 19__ 19__

CHRISTMAS CARD RECORD

Name: _____	Name: _____
Street: _____	Street: _____
City: _____ State: _____	City: _____ State: _____
Country: _____ Zip: _____	Country: _____ Zip: _____
Sent: 19__ 19__ 19__ 19__ 19__	Sent: 19__ 19__ 19__ 19__ 19__
Received: 19__ 19__ 19__ 19__ 19__	Received: 19__ 19__ 19__ 19__ 19__

Name: _____	Name: _____
Street: _____	Street: _____
City: _____ State: _____	City: _____ State: _____
Country: _____ Zip: _____	Country: _____ Zip: _____
Sent: 19__ 19__ 19__ 19__ 19__	Sent: 19__ 19__ 19__ 19__ 19__
Received: 19__ 19__ 19__ 19__ 19__	Received: 19__ 19__ 19__ 19__ 19__

Name: _____	Name: _____
Street: _____	Street: _____
City: _____ State: _____	City: _____ State: _____
Country: _____ Zip: _____	Country: _____ Zip: _____
Sent: 19__ 19__ 19__ 19__ 19__	Sent: 19__ 19__ 19__ 19__ 19__
Received: 19__ 19__ 19__ 19__ 19__	Received: 19__ 19__ 19__ 19__ 19__

Name: _____	Name: _____
Street: _____	Street: _____
City: _____ State: _____	City: _____ State: _____
Country: _____ Zip: _____	Country: _____ Zip: _____
Sent: 19__ 19__ 19__ 19__ 19__	Sent: 19__ 19__ 19__ 19__ 19__
Received: 19__ 19__ 19__ 19__ 19__	Received: 19__ 19__ 19__ 19__ 19__

Name: _____	Name: _____
Street: _____	Street: _____
City: _____ State: _____	City: _____ State: _____
Country: _____ Zip: _____	Country: _____ Zip: _____
Sent: 19__ 19__ 19__ 19__ 19__	Sent: 19__ 19__ 19__ 19__ 19__
Received: 19__ 19__ 19__ 19__ 19__	Received: 19__ 19__ 19__ 19__ 19__

CHRISTMAS CARD RECORD

Name: _____
Street: _____
City: _____ State: _____
Country: _____ Zip: _____
Sent: 19__ 19__ 19__ 19__ 19__
Received: 19__ 19__ 19__ 19__ 19__

Name: _____
Street: _____
City: _____ State: _____
Country: _____ Zip: _____
Sent: 19__ 19__ 19__ 19__ 19__
Received: 19__ 19__ 19__ 19__ 19__

Name: _____
Street: _____
City: _____ State: _____
Country: _____ Zip: _____
Sent: 19__ 19__ 19__ 19__ 19__
Received: 19__ 19__ 19__ 19__ 19__

Name: _____
Street: _____
City: _____ State: _____
Country: _____ Zip: _____
Sent: 19__ 19__ 19__ 19__ 19__
Received: 19__ 19__ 19__ 19__ 19__

Name: _____
Street: _____
City: _____ State: _____
Country: _____ Zip: _____
Sent: 19__ 19__ 19__ 19__ 19__
Received: 19__ 19__ 19__ 19__ 19__

Name: _____
Street: _____
City: _____ State: _____
Country: _____ Zip: _____
Sent: 19__ 19__ 19__ 19__ 19__
Received: 19__ 19__ 19__ 19__ 19__

Name: _____
Street: _____
City: _____ State: _____
Country: _____ Zip: _____
Sent: 19__ 19__ 19__ 19__ 19__
Received: 19__ 19__ 19__ 19__ 19__

Name: _____
Street: _____
City: _____ State: _____
Country: _____ Zip: _____
Sent: 19__ 19__ 19__ 19__ 19__
Received: 19__ 19__ 19__ 19__ 19__

Name: _____
Street: _____
City: _____ State: _____
Country: _____ Zip: _____
Sent: 19__ 19__ 19__ 19__ 19__
Received: 19__ 19__ 19__ 19__ 19__

Name: _____
Street: _____
City: _____ State: _____
Country: _____ Zip: _____
Sent: 19__ 19__ 19__ 19__ 19__
Received: 19__ 19__ 19__ 19__ 19__

CHRISTMAS CARD RECORD

Name: _____	Name: _____
Street: _____	Street: _____
City: _____ State: _____	City: _____ State: _____
Country: _____ Zip: _____	Country: _____ Zip: _____
Sent: 19__ 19__ 19__ 19__ 19__	Sent: 19__ 19__ 19__ 19__ 19__
Received: 19__ 19__ 19__ 19__ 19__	Received: 19__ 19__ 19__ 19__ 19__
Name: _____	Name: _____
Street: _____	Street: _____
City: _____ State: _____	City: _____ State: _____
Country: _____ Zip: _____	Country: _____ Zip: _____
Sent: 19__ 19__ 19__ 19__ 19__	Sent: 19__ 19__ 19__ 19__ 19__
Received: 19__ 19__ 19__ 19__ 19__	Received: 19__ 19__ 19__ 19__ 19__
Name: _____	Name: _____
Street: _____	Street: _____
City: _____ State: _____	City: _____ State: _____
Country: _____ Zip: _____	Country: _____ Zip: _____
Sent: 19__ 19__ 19__ 19__ 19__	Sent: 19__ 19__ 19__ 19__ 19__
Received: 19__ 19__ 19__ 19__ 19__	Received: 19__ 19__ 19__ 19__ 19__
Name: _____	Name: _____
Street: _____	Street: _____
City: _____ State: _____	City: _____ State: _____
Country: _____ Zip: _____	Country: _____ Zip: _____
Sent: 19__ 19__ 19__ 19__ 19__	Sent: 19__ 19__ 19__ 19__ 19__
Received: 19__ 19__ 19__ 19__ 19__	Received: 19__ 19__ 19__ 19__ 19__
Name: _____	Name: _____
Street: _____	Street: _____
City: _____ State: _____	City: _____ State: _____
Country: _____ Zip: _____	Country: _____ Zip: _____
Sent: 19__ 19__ 19__ 19__ 19__	Sent: 19__ 19__ 19__ 19__ 19__
Received: 19__ 19__ 19__ 19__ 19__	Received: 19__ 19__ 19__ 19__ 19__

CHRISTMAS CARD RECORD

Name: _____	Name: _____
Street: _____	Street: _____
City: _____ State: _____	City: _____ State: _____
Country: _____ Zip: _____	Country: _____ Zip: _____
Sent: 19__ 19__ 19__ 19__ 19__	Sent: 19__ 19__ 19__ 19__ 19__
Received: 19__ 19__ 19__ 19__ 19__	Received: 19__ 19__ 19__ 19__ 19__
Name: _____	Name: _____
Street: _____	Street: _____
City: _____ State: _____	City: _____ State: _____
Country: _____ Zip: _____	Country: _____ Zip: _____
Sent: 19__ 19__ 19__ 19__ 19__	Sent: 19__ 19__ 19__ 19__ 19__
Received: 19__ 19__ 19__ 19__ 19__	Received: 19__ 19__ 19__ 19__ 19__
Name: _____	Name: _____
Street: _____	Street: _____
City: _____ State: _____	City: _____ State: _____
Country: _____ Zip: _____	Country: _____ Zip: _____
Sent: 19__ 19__ 19__ 19__ 19__	Sent: 19__ 19__ 19__ 19__ 19__
Received: 19__ 19__ 19__ 19__ 19__	Received: 19__ 19__ 19__ 19__ 19__
Name: _____	Name: _____
Street: _____	Street: _____
City: _____ State: _____	City: _____ State: _____
Country: _____ Zip: _____	Country: _____ Zip: _____
Sent: 19__ 19__ 19__ 19__ 19__	Sent: 19__ 19__ 19__ 19__ 19__
Received: 19__ 19__ 19__ 19__ 19__	Received: 19__ 19__ 19__ 19__ 19__
Name: _____	Name: _____
Street: _____	Street: _____
City: _____ State: _____	City: _____ State: _____
Country: _____ Zip: _____	Country: _____ Zip: _____
Sent: 19__ 19__ 19__ 19__ 19__	Sent: 19__ 19__ 19__ 19__ 19__
Received: 19__ 19__ 19__ 19__ 19__	Received: 19__ 19__ 19__ 19__ 19__

CHRISTMAS CARD RECORD

Name: _____

Street: _____

City: _____ State: _____

Country: _____ Zip: _____

Sent: 19__ 19__ 19__ 19__ 19__

Received: 19__ 19__ 19__ 19__ 19__

Name: _____

Street: _____

City: _____ State: _____

Country: _____ Zip: _____

Sent: 19__ 19__ 19__ 19__ 19__

Received: 19__ 19__ 19__ 19__ 19__

Name: _____

Street: _____

City: _____ State: _____

Country: _____ Zip: _____

Sent: 19__ 19__ 19__ 19__ 19__

Received: 19__ 19__ 19__ 19__ 19__

Name: _____

Street: _____

City: _____ State: _____

Country: _____ Zip: _____

Sent: 19__ 19__ 19__ 19__ 19__

Received: 19__ 19__ 19__ 19__ 19__

Name: _____

Street: _____

City: _____ State: _____

Country: _____ Zip: _____

Sent: 19__ 19__ 19__ 19__ 19__

Received: 19__ 19__ 19__ 19__ 19__

Name: _____

Street: _____

City: _____ State: _____

Country: _____ Zip: _____

Sent: 19__ 19__ 19__ 19__ 19__

Received: 19__ 19__ 19__ 19__ 19__

Name: _____

Street: _____

City: _____ State: _____

Country: _____ Zip: _____

Sent: 19__ 19__ 19__ 19__ 19__

Received: 19__ 19__ 19__ 19__ 19__

Name: _____

Street: _____

City: _____ State: _____

Country: _____ Zip: _____

Sent: 19__ 19__ 19__ 19__ 19__

Received: 19__ 19__ 19__ 19__ 19__

Name: _____

Street: _____

City: _____ State: _____

Country: _____ Zip: _____

Sent: 19__ 19__ 19__ 19__ 19__

Received: 19__ 19__ 19__ 19__ 19__

Name: _____

Street: _____

City: _____ State: _____

Country: _____ Zip: _____

Sent: 19__ 19__ 19__ 19__ 19__

Received: 19__ 19__ 19__ 19__ 19__

CHRISTMAS CARD RECORD

Name: _____

Street: _____

City: _____ State: _____

Country: _____ Zip: _____

Sent: 19__ 19__ 19__ 19__ 19__

Received: 19__ 19__ 19__ 19__ 19__

Name: _____

Street: _____

City: _____ State: _____

Country: _____ Zip: _____

Sent: 19__ 19__ 19__ 19__ 19__

Received: 19__ 19__ 19__ 19__ 19__

Name: _____

Street: _____

City: _____ State: _____

Country: _____ Zip: _____

Sent: 19__ 19__ 19__ 19__ 19__

Received: 19__ 19__ 19__ 19__ 19__

Name: _____

Street: _____

City: _____ State: _____

Country: _____ Zip: _____

Sent: 19__ 19__ 19__ 19__ 19__

Received: 19__ 19__ 19__ 19__ 19__

Name: _____

Street: _____

City: _____ State: _____

Country: _____ Zip: _____

Sent: 19__ 19__ 19__ 19__ 19__

Received: 19__ 19__ 19__ 19__ 19__

Name: _____

Street: _____

City: _____ State: _____

Country: _____ Zip: _____

Sent: 19__ 19__ 19__ 19__ 19__

Received: 19__ 19__ 19__ 19__ 19__

Name: _____

Street: _____

City: _____ State: _____

Country: _____ Zip: _____

Sent: 19__ 19__ 19__ 19__ 19__

Received: 19__ 19__ 19__ 19__ 19__

Name: _____

Street: _____

City: _____ State: _____

Country: _____ Zip: _____

Sent: 19__ 19__ 19__ 19__ 19__

Received: 19__ 19__ 19__ 19__ 19__

Name: _____

Street: _____

City: _____ State: _____

Country: _____ Zip: _____

Sent: 19__ 19__ 19__ 19__ 19__

Received: 19__ 19__ 19__ 19__ 19__

Name: _____

Street: _____

City: _____ State: _____

Country: _____ Zip: _____

Sent: 19__ 19__ 19__ 19__ 19__

Received: 19__ 19__ 19__ 19__ 19__

CHRISTMAS CARD RECORD

Name: _____
Street: _____
City: _____ State: _____
Country: _____ Zip: _____
Sent: 19__ 19__ 19__ 19__ 19__
Received: 19__ 19__ 19__ 19__ 19__

Name: _____
Street: _____
City: _____ State: _____
Country: _____ Zip: _____
Sent: 19__ 19__ 19__ 19__ 19__
Received: 19__ 19__ 19__ 19__ 19__

Name: _____
Street: _____
City: _____ State: _____
Country: _____ Zip: _____
Sent: 19__ 19__ 19__ 19__ 19__
Received: 19__ 19__ 19__ 19__ 19__

Name: _____
Street: _____
City: _____ State: _____
Country: _____ Zip: _____
Sent: 19__ 19__ 19__ 19__ 19__
Received: 19__ 19__ 19__ 19__ 19__

Name: _____
Street: _____
City: _____ State: _____
Country: _____ Zip: _____
Sent: 19__ 19__ 19__ 19__ 19__
Received: 19__ 19__ 19__ 19__ 19__

Name: _____
Street: _____
City: _____ State: _____
Country: _____ Zip: _____
Sent: 19__ 19__ 19__ 19__ 19__
Received: 19__ 19__ 19__ 19__ 19__

Name: _____
Street: _____
City: _____ State: _____
Country: _____ Zip: _____
Sent: 19__ 19__ 19__ 19__ 19__
Received: 19__ 19__ 19__ 19__ 19__

Name: _____
Street: _____
City: _____ State: _____
Country: _____ Zip: _____
Sent: 19__ 19__ 19__ 19__ 19__
Received: 19__ 19__ 19__ 19__ 19__

Name: _____
Street: _____
City: _____ State: _____
Country: _____ Zip: _____
Sent: 19__ 19__ 19__ 19__ 19__
Received: 19__ 19__ 19__ 19__ 19__

Name: _____
Street: _____
City: _____ State: _____
Country: _____ Zip: _____
Sent: 19__ 19__ 19__ 19__ 19__
Received: 19__ 19__ 19__ 19__ 19__

CHRISTMAS CARD RECORD

Name: _____

Street: _____

City: _____ State: _____

Country: _____ Zip: _____

Sent: 19__ 19__ 19__ 19__ 19__

Received: 19__ 19__ 19__ 19__ 19__

Name: _____

Street: _____

City: _____ State: _____

Country: _____ Zip: _____

Sent: 19__ 19__ 19__ 19__ 19__

Received: 19__ 19__ 19__ 19__ 19__

Name: _____

Street: _____

City: _____ State: _____

Country: _____ Zip: _____

Sent: 19__ 19__ 19__ 19__ 19__

Received: 19__ 19__ 19__ 19__ 19__

Name: _____

Street: _____

City: _____ State: _____

Country: _____ Zip: _____

Sent: 19__ 19__ 19__ 19__ 19__

Received: 19__ 19__ 19__ 19__ 19__

Name: _____

Street: _____

City: _____ State: _____

Country: _____ Zip: _____

Sent: 19__ 19__ 19__ 19__ 19__

Received: 19__ 19__ 19__ 19__ 19__

Name: _____

Street: _____

City: _____ State: _____

Country: _____ Zip: _____

Sent: 19__ 19__ 19__ 19__ 19__

Received: 19__ 19__ 19__ 19__ 19__

Name: _____

Street: _____

City: _____ State: _____

Country: _____ Zip: _____

Sent: 19__ 19__ 19__ 19__ 19__

Received: 19__ 19__ 19__ 19__ 19__

Name: _____

Street: _____

City: _____ State: _____

Country: _____ Zip: _____

Sent: 19__ 19__ 19__ 19__ 19__

Received: 19__ 19__ 19__ 19__ 19__

Name: _____

Street: _____

City: _____ State: _____

Country: _____ Zip: _____

Sent: 19__ 19__ 19__ 19__ 19__

Received: 19__ 19__ 19__ 19__ 19__

Name: _____

Street: _____

City: _____ State: _____

Country: _____ Zip: _____

Sent: 19__ 19__ 19__ 19__ 19__

Received: 19__ 19__ 19__ 19__ 19__

CHRISTMAS CARD RECORD

Name: _____	Name: _____
Street: _____	Street: _____
City: _____ State: _____	City: _____ State: _____
Country: _____ Zip: _____	Country: _____ Zip: _____
Sent: 19__ 19__ 19__ 19__ 19__	Sent: 19__ 19__ 19__ 19__ 19__
Received: 19__ 19__ 19__ 19__ 19__	Received: 19__ 19__ 19__ 19__ 19__

Name: _____	Name: _____
Street: _____	Street: _____
City: _____ State: _____	City: _____ State: _____
Country: _____ Zip: _____	Country: _____ Zip: _____
Sent: 19__ 19__ 19__ 19__ 19__	Sent: 19__ 19__ 19__ 19__ 19__
Received: 19__ 19__ 19__ 19__ 19__	Received: 19__ 19__ 19__ 19__ 19__

Name: _____	Name: _____
Street: _____	Street: _____
City: _____ State: _____	City: _____ State: _____
Country: _____ Zip: _____	Country: _____ Zip: _____
Sent: 19__ 19__ 19__ 19__ 19__	Sent: 19__ 19__ 19__ 19__ 19__
Received: 19__ 19__ 19__ 19__ 19__	Received: 19__ 19__ 19__ 19__ 19__

Name: _____	Name: _____
Street: _____	Street: _____
City: _____ State: _____	City: _____ State: _____
Country: _____ Zip: _____	Country: _____ Zip: _____
Sent: 19__ 19__ 19__ 19__ 19__	Sent: 19__ 19__ 19__ 19__ 19__
Received: 19__ 19__ 19__ 19__ 19__	Received: 19__ 19__ 19__ 19__ 19__

Name: _____	Name: _____
Street: _____	Street: _____
City: _____ State: _____	City: _____ State: _____
Country: _____ Zip: _____	Country: _____ Zip: _____
Sent: 19__ 19__ 19__ 19__ 19__	Sent: 19__ 19__ 19__ 19__ 19__
Received: 19__ 19__ 19__ 19__ 19__	Received: 19__ 19__ 19__ 19__ 19__

CHRISTMAS CARD RECORD

Name: _____

Street: _____

City: _____ State: _____

Country: _____ Zip: _____

Sent: 19__   19__   19__   19__   19__

Received: 19__   19__   19__   19__   19__

Name: _____

Street: _____

City: _____ State: _____

Country: _____ Zip: _____

Sent: 19__   19__   19__   19__   19__

Received: 19__   19__   19__   19__   19__

Name: _____

Street: _____

City: _____ State: _____

Country: _____ Zip: _____

Sent: 19__   19__   19__   19__   19__

Received: 19__   19__   19__   19__   19__

Name: _____

Street: _____

City: _____ State: _____

Country: _____ Zip: _____

Sent: 19__   19__   19__   19__   19__

Received: 19__   19__   19__   19__   19__

Name: _____

Street: _____

City: _____ State: _____

Country: _____ Zip: _____

Sent: 19__   19__   19__   19__   19__

Received: 19__   19__   19__   19__   19__

Name: _____

Street: _____

City: _____ State: _____

Country: _____ Zip: _____

Sent: 19__   19__   19__   19__   19__

Received: 19__   19__   19__   19__   19__

Name: _____

Street: _____

City: _____ State: _____

Country: _____ Zip: _____

Sent: 19__   19__   19__   19__   19__

Received: 19__   19__   19__   19__   19__

Name: _____

Street: _____

City: _____ State: _____

Country: _____ Zip: _____

Sent: 19__   19__   19__   19__   19__

Received: 19__   19__   19__   19__   19__

Name: _____

Street: _____

City: _____ State: _____

Country: _____ Zip: _____

Sent: 19__   19__   19__   19__   19__

Received: 19__   19__   19__   19__   19__

Name: _____

Street: _____

City: _____ State: _____

Country: _____ Zip: _____

Sent: 19__   19__   19__   19__   19__

Received: 19__   19__   19__   19__   19__

CHRISTMAS CARD RECORD

Name: _____
Street: _____
City: _____ State: _____
Country: _____ Zip: _____
Sent: 19__ 19__ 19__ 19__ 19__
Received: 19__ 19__ 19__ 19__ 19__

Name: _____
Street: _____
City: _____ State: _____
Country: _____ Zip: _____
Sent: 19__ 19__ 19__ 19__ 19__
Received: 19__ 19__ 19__ 19__ 19__

Name: _____
Street: _____
City: _____ State: _____
Country: _____ Zip: _____
Sent: 19__ 19__ 19__ 19__ 19__
Received: 19__ 19__ 19__ 19__ 19__

Name: _____
Street: _____
City: _____ State: _____
Country: _____ Zip: _____
Sent: 19__ 19__ 19__ 19__ 19__
Received: 19__ 19__ 19__ 19__ 19__

Name: _____
Street: _____
City: _____ State: _____
Country: _____ Zip: _____
Sent: 19__ 19__ 19__ 19__ 19__
Received: 19__ 19__ 19__ 19__ 19__

Name: _____
Street: _____
City: _____ State: _____
Country: _____ Zip: _____
Sent: 19__ 19__ 19__ 19__ 19__
Received: 19__ 19__ 19__ 19__ 19__

Name: _____
Street: _____
City: _____ State: _____
Country: _____ Zip: _____
Sent: 19__ 19__ 19__ 19__ 19__
Received: 19__ 19__ 19__ 19__ 19__

Name: _____
Street: _____
City: _____ State: _____
Country: _____ Zip: _____
Sent: 19__ 19__ 19__ 19__ 19__
Received: 19__ 19__ 19__ 19__ 19__

Name: _____
Street: _____
City: _____ State: _____
Country: _____ Zip: _____
Sent: 19__ 19__ 19__ 19__ 19__
Received: 19__ 19__ 19__ 19__ 19__

Name: _____
Street: _____
City: _____ State: _____
Country: _____ Zip: _____
Sent: 19__ 19__ 19__ 19__ 19__
Received: 19__ 19__ 19__ 19__ 19__

Bibliography

Baldrige, Letitia. *The Amy Vanderbuilt Complete Book of Etiquette*. New York, 1978

Bartlett, John. *Familiar Quotations*. New York, 1980.

Buday, George. *The History of the Christmas Card*. London, 1965.

Crippen, T. G. *Christmas and Christmas Lore*. Chicago, 1970.

Hadfield, Miles and John. *The Twelve Days of Christmas*. Boston, Toronto, 1961.

Hottes, Alfred Carl. *1001 Christmas Facts and Fancies*. New York, 1944.

Miller, Joni and Thompson, Lowry. *The Rubber Stamp Album*. New York, 1978.

Myers, Robert J., ed. *The Complete Book of American Holidays*. New York, 1972.

Sansom, William. *A Book of Christmas*. New York, Toronto, 1968.

Snyder Phillip. *December 25th, The Joys of Christmas Past*. New York, 1985.

Cover design by Robert Howard

Book design by Paul M. Hartloff

Layout and typesetting by Paul M. Hartloff on an Apple Macintosh Computer using Ready, Set, Go by Letraset.

Typeset Output by Port-to-Print, Madison, Wisconsin on a Linotronic 100.

Printed by McNaughton & Gunn, Inc.

The PERFECT Christmas gift for yourself and favorite friends or relatives.

A New Approach to Christmas Greetings!

To order by mail complete the order form and mail. Be sure to verify your address. Include your payment with a personal check or money order. Please do not send cash. We ship by U.P.S. and United States Postal Service depending on location.

Fold here

- INDIVIDUAL ORDER FORM -

A New Approach to Christmas Greetings by ViAnn Oden

Name: _____ Phone: (_____)_____
Area Code

Street: _____

City: _____ State: _____ Zip: _____

Description	Quantity	Total Cost
A New Approach to Christmas Greetings by ViAnn Oden		

Mailing Address	1 copy	2 copies	3 copies	4 copies	Shipping	Shipped to U. S. addresses ONLY!	$1.50
CA (includes tax)	$10.55	$21.10	$31.65	$42.20			
Other states	$9.95	$19.90	$29.85	$39.80		**TOTAL**	

Fold here

ANVIPA PRESS
160-D N. Fairview Ave. Suite 226
Goleta, CA
                   93117

The PERFECT Christmas gift for yourself and favorite friends or relatives.

A New Approach to Christmas Greetings!

To order by mail complete the order form and mail. Be sure to verify your address. Include your payment with a personal check or money order. Please do not send cash. We ship by U.P.S. and United States Postal Service depending on location.

- **Fold here** -

- INDIVIDUAL ORDER FORM -

A New Approach to Christmas Greetings by ViAnn Oden

Name: _____ Phone: (_____)_____
                                                              Area Code

Street: _____

City: _____ State: _____ Zip: _____

Description	Quantity	Total Cost
A New Approach to Christmas Greetings by ViAnn Oden		

Mailing Address	1 copy	2 copies	3 copies	4 copies	Shipping	Shipped to U. S. addresses ONLY!	$1.50
CA (includes tax)	$10.55	$21.10	$31.65	$42.20		**TOTAL**	
Other states	$9.95	$19.90	$29.85	$39.80			

Fold here

ANVIPA PRESS
160-D N. Fairview Ave. Suite 226
Goleta, CA
                93117